Holdfast

Holdfast

At Home in the Natural World

KATHLEEN DEAN MOORE

THE LYONS PRESS

Printed in the United States of America

Designed by Cindy LaBreacht

First Edition

10 9 8 7 6 5 4 3 2 1

Library of Congress Cataloging-in-Publication Data

Moore, Kathleen Dean.

     Holdfast: at home in the natural world / Kathleen Dean Moore.

        p.   cm.

     1. Nature. 2. Human ecology. 3. Moore, Kathleen Dean.

  I. Title.

QH81.M853 1999

508—dc21   98-30763

                      CIP

THESE ESSAYS, several under different titles or in different form, appeared originally in the following:

"The Song of the Canyon Wren," *Interdisciplinary Studies in Literature and the Environment*

"Pale Morning Dun (*Ephemerella infrequens*)," *Southern Review*

"The Prometheus Moth," *Commonweal*

"Traveling the Logging Road, Coast Range," *WildEarth*

"A Field Guide to Western Birds," *California Wild*

"Field Notes for an Aesthetic of Storms," *Bear Essentials*

"Canoeing on the Line of a Song," *Canoe and Kayak*

THIS BOOK IS DEDICATED

to the Deans and the Moores,

my family, my bedrock.

HOLDFAST. *A rootlike structure, as of algae and other simple plants, for attachment to the substrate.*

—*Rachel Carson*

CONTENTS

PROLO𝑔UE

In the green, light-shot sea along the Oregon coast, bullwhip kelp lean toward land on the incoming tides and swirl seaward as the water falls away, never letting go of their grip on the ocean floor. What keeps each plant in place is a holdfast, a fist of knobby fingers that stick to rock with a glue the plant makes from sunshine and salt water, an invisible bond strong enough to hold against all but the worst winter gales. The holdfast is a structure biologists don't entirely understand. Philosophers have not even begun to try.

In blue, halogen-lit places of constant movement, so many of us live in a time of separations—the comings and goings at the turning of the century, the airport embraces, the X-ray rooms, loneliness, notes left by the phone. Children grow tall, then restless. Grandparents grow wise, then forget their children's names. My work takes me from place to place—Ohio, Oregon, Minnesota, Oregon, Alaska, Arizona, British Columbia, Oregon again. Everywhere I go, I pass people who have come from someplace else. We all have left so much behind. Sunday dinners. Front porches. Small certainties. Knowledge of when to plant tomatoes, and where to buy string, and what to do when someone dies. Secret places of safety and meaning—a worn bank beside the creek or a patch of hollyhocks, scratchy with pollen and bees.

We professors, who should be studying connection, study distinctions instead. In white laboratories, biologists find it easy to forget that they are natural philosophers. Philosophers, for their part, pluck ideas out of contexts like worms out of holes, and hold them dangling and drying in bright light. When people lock themselves in their houses at night and seal the windows shut to keep out storms, it is possible to forget, sometimes for years and years, that human beings are part of the natural world. We are only reminded, if we are reminded at all, by a sadness we can't explain and a longing for a place that feels like home.

Sitting on a boulder whitewashed by western gulls, watching the sliding surf, I resolve to study holdfasts. What will we cling to, in the confusion of the tides? What structures of connection will hold us in place? How will we find an attachment to the natural world that makes us feel safe and fully alive, here, at the edge of water?

K.D.M.
Corvallis, Oregon

ACKNOWLEDGMENTS

It is often said that what a writer needs most is time alone to think, to write, to agonize: the writer chewing forlornly on a pencil, or walking snowy streets alone. Don't believe it for a minute.

Frank and I lived by ourselves in an isolated Northwoods cabin last fall—an experiment in the writing life. I learned to build a fire in a cookstove and revise text with my mittens on. But most important, I learned that I can no more write in isolation than build a fire with one log. A fire needs bundles of kindling and at least two logs to hold the heat, which is a lesson for any writer. Even Thoreau walked to town for Sunday lunch with friends. So I am grateful—as a person and as a writer—for my family, friends, and colleagues, for the warmth of their company and the spark of their ideas.

My deep-felt thanks . . .

To Frank, casting dry flies on a day that threatens rain. To Jonathan, who is now, I would guess, asleep on a beach under the

Southern Cross. To Erin, who at last word was wind-bound with her friends on a boundary waters lake. To all the Deans and all the Moores who walked these trails with us, these wise and wonderful people. To my sisters, Sally Swegan and Nancy Rosselli, for their stories and their love. To our backcountry friends, Todd and Susan Brown, who know which way the current flows and how to call in wrens.

To the philosophers and scientists who shared their knowledge and their passion—Marcus Borg, Natasha Calvin, Robert Ellis, Charles King, Robert Mason, Jessica McKibben, Bruce Menge, Frank Moore, James Rose, and Lani Roberts; and to a scientist-philosopher of the first rank, Jonathan Moore.

To writers, generous and talented people who read early drafts and tried to set me straight—Chris Anderson, Marion McNamara, Yvonne Mozee, David Platt, Steve Radosevich, Marjorie Sandor, Carolyn Servid, and Gail Wells. To Maria Deira, a talented research associate and writer, who helped in so many ways during two hot summers. Especially, to a young editor who has a miraculous way with words—Erin Moore. To Victoria Shoemaker of Spieler Agency West, for help and affirmation, and to Lilly Golden of the Lyons Press, for her unfailing faith and good advice.

To George and Amy Somero who shared their cabin, a peaceful place built of knotty pine and family love. To Carolyn Servid and Dorik Mechau, co-directors of the Island Institute, good people of boundless intellect and hospitality.

And always, to the wild places.

Thank you for your gifts.

CONNECTION

THE TESTIMONY *of* THE MARSH

At the upper end of a high desert lake, where spring runoff floods into dwarf willows and marsh grass, the coots are so noisy we don't even try to talk. Two males lower their heads, run across the water, and charge at each other. Butting chests, they start to kick-fight. It apparently isn't easy to kick when you're a coot on water, but they flop and jump, falling on their backs, trying to grab with one foot and smack with the other. The noise is awful; hooting like gorillas, they splash their wings and slap their feet until they are hidden behind a screen of spray. The Canada geese pretend they don't notice. The gander swims between his goslings and the coots, a parent herding his children through Times Square. But the yellow-headed blackbirds have no such inhibitions. "Wow," they say. "Wow." Frank and I, entirely without shame, sit in the canoe and study the coots with binoculars.

Suddenly the fight is over. The coots turn their backs and in utmost contempt, lift their wings as if they were shirttails and moon each other. On their little duckish backsides are two big white dots. Their feathers are ruffled, their foreheads are swollen, and they never stop yacking, a sound that carries all the way across the lake. Nothing in the world matters to a coot, it would seem, but to carry on like this all night.

Usually western grebes are stately birds with long white necks and a thoughtful look. But this evening, they've got their necks bent so far back their foreheads touch their tails, displaying a gorgeous arc of white throat. Then, just when we think they will turn a backward somersault with the effort to show off, two grebes come together. They lift their heads, stretch their necks to great heights, rise on frantically paddling feet, and rush side by side toward open water, their arched necks as high and proud as prancing stallions. Then they slow, sink, and dive underwater. "Wow," say the yellow-headed blackbirds.

There must be thousands of yellow-heads, each one tilting and swaying on a high branch of a willow thicket, yellow feathers all fluffed out and wings lifted to display blazing white patches and broad shoulders. Chasing, preening, threatening, posturing, showing off, yelling a call that sounds like "shut up," but never shutting up—it's a nonstop display of rudeness, insults and imprecations, harsh throaty challenges that go on and on. I feel like a playground supervisor in the midst of all this mischief. Somewhere up in the sky, a snipe is carving enormous arcs, its wings whinnying in the wind.

The amount of energy devoted to all this aggression and sex and territoriality is astounding. And this says nothing of the swal-

THE TESTIMONY OF THE MARSH / 21

lows, who dive by and snatch insects off the water, or perch, chattering, on a strand of barbed wire stretched over the marsh. Sometimes two swallows separate from the others, fly high in the air, fussing around each other, and then fall together. As they fall, they flutter their wings so they descend in a close spiral, their bodies repeatedly coming together with the lightest touch, a kiss. It's the most beautiful mating display I have ever seen, and we turn the canoe to get another look at the softness of the touch, the breathtaking plunge, the fluttering fall, the spiral, the dance of falling. And then there is another pair, falling, fluttering, coming together, and just as their wing-tips touch the water, soaring off in different directions. The soft hills on the far side of the lake reflect on water roiled and mussed by waterfowl intent on their purposes, all sound and fury, concentrating with deadly earnest on the business at hand. The noise charges the air like electricity.

And then the frogs switch on. First there is the sawing soprano line of the tree frogs, *kreck-ek kreck-ek.* The red-legged frogs' calls are deeper, regular on a one-two count, a low-throated *GRACK-grick* that seems to come from the near edge of the marsh. The lake is a riot, an orchestra of lunatics warming up. All the nighttime hoots and clacks and sighs and squeaks. An eared grebe pops up next to the canoe. He looks us over with a glowing red eye. A fan of golden feathers flares back from both sides of his brow. The grebe bobs its head and raises its elbows to threaten us. Does he want to fight the canoe? Then he takes another look, ducks his head, somersaults into the water, and disappears. A dozen mergansers beat against the water and flap into the night. Yellow fades out of the sky. The marsh, at last, grows quiet.

All this raucous celebration of health and life and love and beauty, every ounce of attention and strength focused on this business of carrying on—it stops our paddles and leaves us breathless and rejoicing. Uproarious, raging life. What does it mean?

Every now and then, a student in my philosophy class will raise The Question. Clearly embarrassed to ask what seems like a parody of all questions, he plunges in anyway. What is all this for? What does it signify? What is the *meaning* of life?

It's usually an easy enough question to evade. Professors get pretty glib, and there are lots of gambits, and these days philosophy is mostly about language anyway, and you can usually turn the question back on the student or tell him that if he has to ask, he probably won't be satisfied with the answer. And then the words trail off and students shift in their seats, impatient to move back to material that will be on the test.

But last week, a student who had studied metaphysics and epistemology and Søren Kierkegaard, the student who read Immanuel Kant and brought fresh fruit to class, killed herself with a single gunshot to the head, sitting at home, at the kitchen table. She left no note, no explanation, and no one can make any sense of it. Her professors lean heavily against the classroom walls and cannot speak. We realize too late that we never taught our students what ducks know without knowing, that "we must love life before loving its meaning," as Dostoyevsky told us. We must love life, and some meaning may grow from that love. But "if love of life disappears, no meaning can console us."

What is it all for, this magnifying-glass-in-the-sun focus on being, this marshland, this wetness, this stewpot, this great splashing and thrusting, this determination among the willows, the flare-up, the colors, the plumage, the effort, the noise, the complexity that leaves no note?

Nothing, I think, *except* to continue.

This is the testimony of the marsh: Life directs all its power to one end, and that is to continue to be. A marsh at nightfall is life loving itself. Nothing more. But nothing less, either, and we should not be fooled into thinking this is a small thing.

HOLD*f*AST

The sea otters at the coast aquarium drifted slowly in the currents, floating on their backs with their eyes closed and their hands clasped across their bellies. One bumped against a kelp, then gently rotated and drifted away. Another floated around the tank until its feet bumped into the wall. It ran a hand over its face and went back to sleep, peacefully pivoting across the bay. I made my way to where my daughter was watching the otters from an underwater viewing window. Silhouetted against white fog, the otters appeared as dark shapes drifting unmoored. I wondered how they ever got to sleep, resting on something as insubstantial as salt water. To slide unconscious on a shifting surface that carries you out to sea—it's a human's nightmare. Do the otters wake up startled in an unknown place, with no home port and no influence on the direction of the tides, with only the entangling kelp to keep them from drifting down the coast or washing up on rocks?

[25]

I wanted to gather the otters in my arms, bring them to shore, and wrap blankets around them. A sleeping otter, a sleeping child, moves me deeply, dim light spreading from the open door on the face of a child kept only by some miracle from falling through the surface of the earth.

I looked over at my daughter, who had just turned twenty-four. "What are you thinking about?" I asked.

"My carburetor," she replied.

I didn't like the idea of getting in one car while she got in another, waving good-bye at some gas-station crossroads, and simply driving off in different directions. But Frank and I were leaving for a camping trip along the Pacific coast, and Erin was heading for Boston. She had given herself two weeks to cross the country, move into her new apartment, and start her first job. Already her car was pinging under the weight of what she thought she would need for her new place—books and music and a rack of spices, binoculars, a giraffe lamp, and a pet scorpion named Buddy.

This will never work, I had said. If we all cut our connections to home, how can we keep our connections with each other? But there was nothing to worry about, Erin had said; our answering machine wasn't going anywhere. Each day she would call to check in, and we could call the machine to pick up her messages. As long as there was a message, we would know she was safe for another day. We could take comfort at least in that, imagining the dark shape of her car drifting slowly across the continent, windows open, heater jammed to high, tape deck pouring country-western music into currents of cold air.

That first afternoon, we called our message machine from a pay phone at the Dairy Queen in Reedsport. "Hi. I'm in Richland at Aunt Nancy's," Erin's voice said. "So far so good. The wind was fierce in the Gorge, but you should have seen the eagles!" I called her aunt's house but no, she had gone out, her uncle said. "But hey, she ate a good dinner, so don't worry."

Frank and I drove on and set up camp next to an island of shore pines in the dunes. All that night, wind gusted in the trees and sand rained on the tent. By morning, the dunes had moved a few inches inland, uncovering old driftwood and burying beach grass in loose sand. I walked the beach to see what the storm tide had left behind. Windrows of by-the-wind sailors. Clumps of mussels, blue and stony. The torn body of a common murre, its head drawn back, its throat exposed, its feathers touched with foam. Herring gulls pecked at detritus tumbled in the high-tide line, and sand fleas popped and clicked, snapping up and falling back, making the sand tremble. At the highest reach of the surf, I found a stranded bullwhip kelp, a rope thirty feet from its flat fronds and air bladder to the holdfast at the end of its stem. The holdfast clung to a broken chunk of bedrock.

I turned the holdfast over in my hand. Each winter, mature kelp plants shed thousands of spores that drift off in the currents, gradually settling on the ocean floor. Wherever a spore lands—on a cobble or a pile of broken shells or on bedrock—it grows strong green fingers that hold on tight, while the plant grows quickly toward the light. In this narrow subtidal zone, where ebbing tides pull the kelp toward the dark sea and storm tides threaten to toss it onto shore, holding on is everything. But what can you cling to, when even bedrock gives way to the tide? What will connect my daughter to a place where she belongs, this daughter who is driving east, holding tightly to the steering wheel of her car?

Carefully over algae-slicked rocks and mussel beds, I picked my way among tidal pools, stopping to pry at a patch of crustal algae spreading across stone like pink paint, an alga reduced to nothing but the capacity to stay in place. A green anemone flinched when I touched it, and suddenly I understood that all the plants and animals at my feet, the periwinkles, the urchins, the acorn barnacles and rock-wrack, all of them have evolved ways to hold against the surf—thousands of tube feet on a single starfish, suction-cup stomachs for gastropods, tufts of black hairs to hold the mussels, bony tubes, sticky feet, and calcified plates. What chance do we have, we humans, born with two feet and an imagination light as a bird?

When I was a child, I couldn't bear to leave home. If our family went for a week's vacation—to a cabin in a beech-maple woods or the shore of Lake Erie—it was always the same. I would lie in the backseat of the car, feverishly, desperately homesick. Even now, I sometimes get that same feeling when I am away from home. It's a kind of emptiness, as if my ribs have sprung a leak, and when I try to breathe, there's nothing to hold in the air. Back then, I tried to stay overnight at my friends' houses, settling myself on the floor in a roll of blankets, but it was no use. Late at night, when the other children started to slide into sleep, I would get up, holding the blankets around me, awaken whatever mother was nearby, and tell her I had to go home. Are you sick? she would ask—a startled mother's standard response. No, I would answer. I just have to go home. My house was always locked, and I rang the doorbell so my parents would let me in. While I waited, I leaned my cheek against the white siding of the only place I belonged, and listened to the screen door open with a squeak I knew by heart.

But our children dart from one continent to another, changing time zones and airplanes as easily as they change their clothes. Our son was in Mexico, but he's on his way to Australia. Erin has just returned from Greece. Sometimes, I don't know where they are for days. I look at the constellations and try to imagine what the stars look like from the southern hemisphere. Our house has the worn edges of a turnpike motel.

"Give our kids roots, and let them have wings," urges the poster on the inside of my kitchen cabinet, and I read the admonishment with increasing horror, imagining a winged and rooted chimera, an osprey, its overgrown talons grotesquely entangled in rocks and root balls, its wings reaching for air, an osprey struggling to be skyborne but held to the ground by all the connections, flapping desperately, almost tearing itself apart with the effort—this creature rooted firmly to the ground and capable of great flight. Sometimes I don't even know what to hope for my children.

"Hi. This is me. You won't believe this. My car conked out in the Rockies and these guys from the park towed me to Bear Lodge. There are no rooms because tomorrow is opening day of deer season, but the waitress says if worse comes to worse, I can sleep on the couch in the bar, so I really lucked out. It's gorgeous here—you can smell the aspens—and the hunters are buying the beer. So, don't worry. Love you. Bye."

I sat on driftwood and imagined sea otters in deep dusk, washing their faces, getting ready for bed on the sea. An otter reaches for a single strand of kelp and lays it across its stomach. In this unreliable embrace, it goes to sleep.

When Erin was learning to walk, we went on penny hikes around our neighborhood, flipping a coin at each corner to decide which way to go, coming home in late afternoon sun that flared through sweet-gum trees and caught in her hair. She learned east from west at the corner where Jackson Street points to the sun falling behind Mary's Peak. She learned to read a map driving red-cinder roads through lodgepole pines at night. But on five-lane inbound Boston highways, will she know where she is? Will she remember what she's made of?—the minerals from lava-flows that strengthen her bones, the salmon, the winter rain that pushes through her heart. Will the salty smell of Boston Harbor remind her of the times she sat in blowing beach grass, leaning against her father's back?

This much I know: Humans don't have holdfasts or suction-cup stomachs, but we do have hearts and minds. We have strong memories of smells that have held meaning for us since we were small, smells that fill us with joy or bring us to our knees with sorrow and regret. Certain sounds go straight to our hearts—seagulls, wind over water, a child's voice, a hymn. We recognize landscapes the way we recognize faces we haven't seen for many years, and greet them with the same embrace and grieve for them when they are gone. You can put down roots by staying in one place. But my hope for my daughter is that there is another way to be deeply and joyously connected to the land even while she's on the move, a way for Erin to feel at home in the natural world, no matter where she is. It's a kind of rootedness that has to do with noticing, with caring, with remembering, with embracing, with rejoicing in the breadth of the horizon and taking comfort in the familiar smell of rain. In the sliding, shifting world my daughter lives in, this may be the closest thing to bedrock.

Somewhere south of Tillamook Bay the next day, we pulled into a gas station on the east side of a little lake. There was fog along the coast, muffling the sunset, but between there and where we stood, the lake lay calm, a watercolor of clouds disturbed now and then by rings like raindrops on the water. At the edge of the lake, a little girl waded in a shallow bay. Pink light reflected off the plane of her cheek. Ordinary people in baseball caps, people with dogs snuffing around their feet, people with children of their own, stood around on the boat ramp while my daughter slept in a motel someplace in Ohio or Pennsylvania or New York, while the lights of passing trucks swept across her face. In a phone booth littered with broken glass, I pressed the numbers of the answering machine in Erin's new apartment to leave a message that would be there when she arrived. "Welcome home," I said, and I had trouble finding air enough for two simple words.

HOWLING WITH STRANGERS

All 128 of us want to hear a wolf howl. So we are overflowing the bleachers and crowding around the edges of a room facing a picture window. Children sit on their heels under the window, their noses pressed against the glass. A young woman bounds in, wearing a plastic name tag like flight attendants wear. "Hi, I'm Cheri, your wolf specialist, and I'll be talking to you today about our wolf ambassadors." She is carrying a plastic tub filled with props: a gray wolf pelt, the skin from its face pressed flat, its eyes squeezed shut, its nose cracking off. A black wolf pelt. The leg bone of a moose. "Seven bites is all it takes for a wolf to crack through this bone," she says. We gasp—the bone's as thick and white as firewood. She has a plaster mold of the pawprint of a wolf, "as big as my hand with the fingers curled in," Cheri says. She holds up the mold and then holds up her hand, the fingers curled in. We gasp again—that big!

The wolves lounge around in front of the window, penned in by a hurricane fence that we can see plainly through the trees. They look a lot like dogs to me, but I don't know what I expected. I can't imagine one of those things circling menacingly around a moose. But maybe the wolves aren't that impressed with us, either. If they are looking through the window, the wolves will see the flat-nosed children, of course, and a German TV crew—tall young men charging around, jostling for position—and rows and rows of people much like myself—middle-aged, middle-income, middle-American, middle-weight and holding. Like a raisin in all that pudding, there is a thin man with waist-length bronze hair holding a baby in a porkpie hat.

We pass the moose bone from hand to hand, up and down the rows. Then a deer's leg with the fur and hoof still attached, the knee tendons blackened and curled. Here comes the black wolf pelt, its legs dragging out behind. The passing is solemn, silent, disconnected from any meaning that I can determine, like some ancient rite.

Cheri talks cheerily. "We have four wolf ambassadors," and she starts to name them: Lakota, Lucas . . . Behind her voice, we hear a distant fire engine. Suddenly, a wolf jumps to the top of a rock, lifts its head, and begins to howl. It's a reedy sound like a clarinet, rising and falling away in a minor key. The sound silences Cheri, who stands still, smiling. The siren wails and another wolf joins in, so it's a trio now—two wolves and a fire engine—*a-wooee, a-wooee, a-wooee.* Some people start to laugh, but stop themselves—this is supposed to be serious stuff. The man with the hair has his eyes closed and his chin up; he looks like he's having a religious experience. For its part, the wolf stands on the rock in a classic pose, pointing its muzzle to the sky as if it has seen its own promotional T-shirts. Every time Cheri starts to talk, the wolves and the fire engine kick in, howling, and drown her out. Everyone is smiling.

I think we have heard wolves howl before, Frank and I, from our bed. When we first came to the Minnesota woods, we asked about wolves at the national forest headquarters. The young woman there wanted to help. "Oh yes, you can hear them everywhere, even in the center of town. They'll be far away, of course, but you can hear them." Then she lowered her voice. "They may not sound like what you think wolves sound like. They sound like violins. So if you wake up in the middle of the night and you hear violins, don't go back to sleep." Sure enough, that very night, we heard the sound of a single violin. We elbowed each other, then we lay stiff in the dark, our eyes wide, big smiles on our faces.

Don't ask me why this is so important. Don't ask me why we are now standing with a half dozen strangers outside the Wolf Center on a clear and icy night, dressed in everything we own, starting with pajamas, ending with fleecy ear-flapped hats, waiting for the wolf communication expert. We are going out to howl for wolves. It costs us seven dollars apiece, prepaid.

This wolf guy's name is Jim, and he bundles us into a white van, telling us the rules—wear your seat belt; sign the liability waiver; when we get to the woods, absolute silence—don't slam the doors or rustle your clothes or scrape the gravel, and do just what you are told. So now we are standing in pitch dark at the end of a dirt road deep in the northwoods, eight strangers standing around the van in absolute silence on a clear, cold night—hugging ourselves, making our feet stay still, listening. After a time, the silence becomes a presence, then a kind of itching.

"Okay," Jim says in a stage whisper. "I'll start, because the alpha-wolf always starts, and then, when you're ready, join in. We'll pack-howl for two minutes, then listen." I expected to feel embarrassed, howling with strangers, or humiliated, relegated without a vote to beta-wolf status, or omega. But what I feel instead is the silence. How will it be possible to begin? Jim stands quiet for a few more minutes.

Finally, he leans over, takes an enormous breath, cups his hands to his mouth, leans back, and begins to howl. The tone of an oboe rises slowly like the crest of a dark wave, slips, falls away in deep liquid sound. Entirely different from the wail of the caged wolves, the song is as dark as the night, or the night is as deep and beautiful as the song—I don't know which. But now it's time for the beta-wolves. I cup my hands to my mouth, suck in my breath, and yowl like a stuck cat. A woman deep inside a ruffed hood howls mournfully, her voice heaving with melodramatic sobs. Frank barks behind me.

Jim has told us to work for discordance. Wolves in a pack will each howl on a different pitch, letting invader packs count their numbers, and sometimes wolves will switch keys in the middle of the howl, to give the impression that each one is several wolves. We work at it, starting our yappy howls on different pitches, but as the group howl draws out at the end, we find that we have tuned ourselves into a minor chord. We try again, yowling discordantly, and again we drift into something Bach would recognize, a rich Lutheran chord. It's as if we can't help ourselves, as if harmony is part of our nature. Jim cuts us off with a wave of his arm against the stars—the conductor of the galaxy choir.

Silence.

Then, off in the distance, we hear a tiny little, cracked howlette—unmistakably a pup. And answering that, a deep-throated, authoritative howl from far away. The pup shuts up. Some of us start to laugh silently, our shoulders jiggling, but now we freeze: There are footsteps in the bushes. A soft step, a cracking twig, a long pause, then step, step, step—stealthy in the dark.

"Sometimes a wolf will walk right up to us," Jim whispers. I contemplate this possibility, measuring the distance to the van. Suddenly, Jim starts to whine and pant and scuff the gravel. I almost jump out of my skin. He pants some more. "Sometimes this draws them in. Nobody move." Nobody move? Is he kidding? He's thrashing around like some wounded animal and he expects us to stand there? What if it *is* a wolf? What if it's a bear? All my instincts signal, flee. Peer pressure pins me to the spot.

Eventually, when nothing materializes, Jim piles us back in the van and we move to a clearing at the center of a marsh where we disperse into the darkness on a dirt track. By now, the sky is so black and the Milky Way so bright that it casts its reflection on the water. There is a yellow glow to the north and as we watch, fingers of light reach into the sky, silhouetting the edge of forest. Every pine cuts the shape of a wolf sitting on its haunches, its nose raised to the sky, silently howling. We are encircled by silent wolf-pines. It's very, very cold.

Jim starts first, his clear oboe tones, then the rest of us, cutting loose, howling at the wolves, at the northern lights, at the big black sea of night, at the bright hole of Arcturus, at Venus, at how far we are from town, at the idea of standing in the dark in the road, howling with strangers. And then suddenly there is a multitude of voices—barking and howling and yapping and carrying on like a drunken riot in wolf-town—a full pack-howl coming from behind the wolf-trees. We stop yowling, transfixed. The ruckus rises to a fever pitch and abruptly dies. Silence washes in, final and infinitely deep.

Nobody moves. Nobody talks. We stand together in the road and listen to the night. I love these people. I don't know a thing about them, but I love them. I want to move close to them and exchange big woolen hugs, ear-flaps pressing against cold noses, mittens patting padded backs. And maybe the wolves would join in, jumping around us, chittering, licking our faces while northern lights flicker and stars tick and the wind jangles with the smell of the marsh. Then maybe all the voices of the universe will come together in a harmonic chord that we can hear if we only listen. It is possible, I think—not likely, but possible—and I stand still, smiling in the dark.

A FIELD GUIDE TO WESTERN BIRDS

My son reads field guides at the breakfast table, leaning over his bowl and scooping cereal into his mouth while he scans the color plates of banded snakes or studies the pawprints of cats in snow. He will study the same set of drawings for long minutes, absorbing the differences between stingrays and sharks. Or he will read a field guide late into the night, cover to cover, as if it were a novel—taking sides with the predators, imagining himself part of each small plot, turning pages all the way to the end, then rereading the first page and dropping the book on the floor. Field guides lie in heaps under his bed—*A Field Guide to Western Birds, Shells of the Pacific Coast and Hawaii, A Field Guide to Western Reptiles and Amphibians, The Pacific Coast Fishes,* and now, *The Field Guide to Eastern Birds,* a gift for high school graduation.

Most of the field guides are small, clothbound books, about the color of dried moss. We call the books by their authors' names, as if they were our grandfathers. "Should we bring Peterson?" we ask. "Somebody remember to pick up Murie before we go." The covers are worn, the fabric corners ground into the cardboard as if someone had taken sandpaper to them. The pages are stiff and wrinkled—*The Field Guide to Rocks and Minerals* carried ten feet by a flash flood, *North American Mammals* left on a rock in the snow. In our *Field Guide to Western Birds,* the pages describing ducks are smudged with black streaks, because when you sit at the edge of a marsh late in the evening while ducks whistle in and drop onto the pond with the sound of a canoe paddle pulling water, midges swarm to the pages of the bird book, their bodies small and soft as ashes. If you brush them away, they smear across the page.

> *Pintail.* Anas acuta. *Male Pintails are slender white-breasted ducks with slim necks, quite different in cut from other ducks of ponds and marshes. They have long, needle-pointed tails.* . . . *Habitat: Marshes, prairies, grainfields, fresh ponds, lakes, salt bays.*
> —*Roger Tory Peterson,* A Field Guide to Western Birds

Some of the books on my shelf—the fern book, the lichen book, the *Field Guide to Ponds and Streams*—had been my mother's. She was a person who exulted in natural facts, who greeted frogs as old friends and rejoiced to find in the forest something she had known only as a picture in a book. The first mayapple in spring, a glimpse of Scorpio crawling claw over claw into the sky above darkened mountains, the first sighting of a vermilion fly-catcher—any of these would fill her with what Joseph Wood Krutch called "the joy we cannot analyze." "*Imagine* living in the same world as the scissor-tailed flycatcher," she would say. *Imagine.* The word always sounded as if it were throwing open its arms. A painted bunting. A blue skink. Elephant flowers, with pink elephant heads spiraling up a stalk in a high mountain meadow. Marshes full of skunk cabbage, smelling like lemonade. If these things can exist, then nothing is impossible. "That's the ticket," she would say.

Among my mother's things, I found a bird book that my son had written for her when he was four. On the first page, he had printed, "LOVE JON," except that he spelled it NOJ and there was a smiley face cradled in the curve of the J. He had drawn a dozen birds with large-scale swoops of a marking pen he held in his fist. Then he brought the drawings to me and told me what words to write. *The Two-Sets-of-Wings Bird and the Hundred-Sets-of-Wings Bird. The big one is trying to swoop down on the little one and he is trying to sneak away. He has four legs.*

Page after page, the birds line up: The Tufted Striped Hawk. The Sharp-toothed Duck. The Rocket Turkey Hawk. The Tufted Pelican-Pelican. The Tiny Sandpiper. All the waterbirds stand on sturdy stalklike legs. But the hawks! Legs shoot out behind diving hawks like exhaust from rockets, or they string out taut as piano wire, or trail under the birds like the crumpled legs of a dead crane fly. All the birds look as though they have on yellow boots, and some of the boots seem to be on fire. The joy we cannot analyze.

I once asked my son what it is about field guides. It's like a dream coming true, he had said. You read about a bird, say, and for years you hold it in your mind. It's an image, a drawing, length and wingspan—that's it. A picture in your mind. But all the time you think, Maybe someday I will see that really. The real thing. And then, someday, you do. And what was just an idea, it comes true. Like a wish.

The fern book has my mother's signature on the title page and, between pages 109 and 110 (LADY FERN *Athyrium filix-femina*), the tip of a fern frond, folded back on itself and pressed flat and dry. Her field book of ponds and streams was published in 1930, when she would have been seventeen. I open the book to the first plate, a softly washed watercolor of a stream and its little life, all overlaid by a piece of tissue paper on which the plants and animals are sketched in ink and number-coded to a list. *Winter life in a brook: a section through swift flowing shallows. 1, stonefly; 2, water cress; 3, alga; 4, sponge gemmules; 5, caddis worm; 6, planarian; . . . 10, dusky salamander.*

I haven't looked at this page in—how many?—fifteen years, and still I recognize the overhanging willows, the glint on the water, the feathery gills of the salamander. I turn to figure 18, a diagram of all the things that live on the underside of a lily pad— the eggs of a whirligig beetle, dragonfly larvae. I remember watch- ing my mother take Jon by the hand and wade knee-deep into a marsh, rejoicing to see a dragonfly split up the back and crawl out of its shuck, bent and damp. With a plastic bucket, they dredged for water boatmen and fairy shrimp. I leaf on through the book and by the time I get to bryozoans, *clustered on the surface of large masses of jelly which . . . hang from twigs,* I have to close the book to keep from being swamped by all the memories.

Spring peeper (Hyla crucifer). *Spring peepers cling to dead grassblades by the pond-side uttering their shrill peeping, one of the earliest calls of spring in the ponds and marshes. They begin*

to sing in March, when the spotted salamander is laying its
eggs, and continue through May. After that they scatter through
swamps and meadows and are only occasionally seen.
    —*Ann Morgan,* Field Book of Ponds and Streams

Lessons from my father are woven into the dichotomous keys at the beginning of every field guide. He was a taxonomist in his professional life and had a taxonomist's view of the world. *Are the plants free-floating on still water, or are they not? Are the stems jointed and hollow, or are they not? Are the leaves entire, or are they variously divided?* And so it goes, in sets of disjunctive syllogisms. Every creature in the whole of the natural world, every scaled or furry or slimish, beetle-backed, high-flying, zero- to hundred-legged creature of night skies or ocean bottoms or mountain sunlight, can be identified in twenty questions, if you get the questions right. *Is it now or has it ever been alive, or not? If living, is it animal, or something else? If an animal, warm-blooded or cold?* One step at a time. Twenty discriminations. "So how many kinds of things are there in the world?" I once asked my father. He pulled his slide rule out of its sheath and computed two to the twentieth power. "One million forty-eight thousand five hundred and seventy-six," he said.

A few years ago, my father gave his grandchildren a special legacy—a hand lens on a leather thong and the logic of the dichotomous key. I remember the exact day. Arriving at our house after a cross-country flight, he immediately changed into jeans and pulled the *Handbook of Northwestern Plants* out of his suitcase. He called for his granddaughter. He called for his grandson and a flower. Then, step by step, he slowly keyed out the flower. This or that. This or that. This or that, until everyone was convinced beyond any doubt that this was an *Ipomopsis aggregata*. Then, reaching out his arms, he pulled the children close to him and each of them in turn keyed out the flower, then another, until he was sure they could do it right.

A gift of rationality. A faith in order. Gratitude for the glory and beauty of a natural world that allows itself to be arranged by reason. A cause for great rejoicing: to wake up every morning knowing that whatever you encounter in the natural world will yield to Linnaeus's two-name scheme, genus and species, a scheme based on the premise that order constrains the violent world of natural creation, that everything in the world relates in predictable ways to everything else. There are no freaks. No miracles. A family for everyone, even *Ursus horribilis:* the terrible bear. A genus, a genesis, a genius. Within that, a specification—a species.

This fact, my father said, should make us tremble with wonder every day of our lives. You can't take the planet for granted; it could all be otherwise. There must be worlds spinning on the far side of Jupiter where field guides are futile, where nothing is this or that, but rather nothing at all or everything at once. Imagine a simple world where everything is one kind of thing, evenly distributed, like red cinders blown out of a red cinder cone onto an even plain, so when the wind blows across the roughness, it plays a single endless note. Cinders and one sound—nothing more. Imagine a planet where no two things are ever the same and there are infinitely many things, a planet where you could not play twenty questions because there are no dichotomies, no regularities, no repeated patterns: one of each, and nothing like anything else. Or imagine a world where chaos never yielded to creation, a world forever unsorted, spinning in the glare that is all light combined. These are worlds that rationality cannot conquer.

So the great miracle is not that conditions on earth permit life to evolve, my father told us, but that conditions on earth permit field guides.

Carry a field guide out of the library, out through the old cross-and-bible front door, across the mowed lawn and into the field, the open country, to the edge of the marsh and to the edge of the sea, to the edge of the night sky, to the edge, and then into the wilderness, where—even there—a book will tell you how to make sense of what you encounter.

> *6A. Adults with protruding upper jaw teeth—felt by stroking tip of salamander's snout from below, while holding its mouth closed; toes often with squarish tips. Climbing Salamanders, Pl. 6.*
> *6B. Teeth rarely protrude; toe tips round. Woodland Salamanders, Pl. 5.*
> *—Robert Stebbins,* A Field Guide to Western Reptiles
> and Amphibians

Most days, I feel safe and comfortable in the rational world my father described, but sometimes it makes me restless, and I turn back toward my mother. When we were growing up, my sisters and I would often come across a flower we didn't know. "What is this?" we would ask. My father would touch the flower gently under its chin. "Some *Ranunculus,*" he would answer. A short pause while he studied the sky over the mountains. "*Ranunculus glaberrimus.*" A chorus of boos from his children. "The real name! What is the real name?" "That *is* the real name," he would insist, but my mother knew better. "It's a buttercup," she would say, and give my father a dirty look, and we would be satisfied. Buttercup was exactly right. Although we would accuse my father of making up gibberish-ranunculish names to suit himself, we never doubted the names my mother gave, no matter how improbable or flamboyant they were—pussytoes, morning glories, whimbrels and whippoorwills, farewell-to-spring, love-lies-bleeding, and the fiery searcher.

Does the world match the capacities of our minds, or do our poor minds limit what is possible for us to know about the world? Maybe our minds do the best they can, capturing what is slow, wounded, common, but missing the best part. The possibility of something beyond human capacity to see makes me wild with frustration, like a dog racing back and forth in front of a closed door, scratching, sniffing air that comes through the crack at the bottom. What is out there that is invisible because it does not match our categories? What exists beyond the visible spectrum, beyond the audible range, outside binomial nomenclature, so glorious that it would blind us, blow out our senses, knock us to the ground?

Fiery Searcher "Caterpillar Hunter" (Calosoma scrutator). Description: Black beetle with dark greenish gold on sides of head and prothorax. Bluish luster on femora. Elytra edged with gold. Reddish hair inside curved middle tibiae. Habitat: Gardens, crop fields, and open woods.
—The Audubon Society Field Guide
to North American Insects and Spiders

It is important to me that my children can distinguish a vulture from a golden eagle by the cant of its wings. It reassures me to know that they can recognize the evening call of robins and the morning call of doves, that they know from its tracks whether a rabbit is coming or going, that they always know which way is west. I want them to go out into a rational world where order gives them pleasure and comfort, but also an improbable world, wild with sound and extravagant with color, where there is always a chance they will find something rare and very beautiful, something that is not in the book.

THE THINg ABOUT DOGS

have never liked dogs. One. They drool. Whenever you sit down,
here comes a dog to rest its chin on your knee and leave behind
a glistening tracery of saliva, like a tent caterpillar or something.
Two. They smell like dogs. Three. They do uncivilized things,
like lie on their backs, twist themselves up, and lick their own
tail ends, setting a bad example. So we have never had dogs. Our
pets have always been things like lizards and water striders and,
until recently, Buddy the Scorpion—clean, cold-blooded, self-
respecting animals.

However, when I was growing up in Ohio, our family had a
dog. Her name was Pixie, which is impossible to understand, since
she was a stubby, fat beagle. My sister says that when her children
are unhappy in that lonely time before sleep, they ask for Pixie stories. But it is beyond me how this provides any comfort at all. Here
is Pixie, following us to school, ensuring that one of us will be

late—because no matter how much we yell "Go home, Pixie," one of us will have to grab her, lift her scrabbling and squirming, run home to shut her in the house, and run back to school, hearing the tardy bell ring when we are still two blocks away, running with a desperation that still comes back in dreams. So what stories does my sister tell her children? I'll have to remember to ask her, but maybe I don't want to know, since this is the sister who called in her own dog when her youngest child vomited into the bottom dresser drawer.

So I was not especially happy when, after the children were in college, Frank and I moved into this sabbatical house on the Wyoming prairie and found that it came complete with three dogs. Spike, an arthritic old black lab who lost an eye in an attack on a badger. Duke, a dalmatian. And Rocky, a young German shepherd with an extra set of claws halfway up its back legs like a rooster, and with a rooster's view of himself. These dogs are always around. When I take my work to the picnic table, I feel like I'm sitting in a dog mortuary—three dogs laid out stiff in the sun, their eyes closed and their tongues hanging out, barely breathing. When I go for a walk along a bridle trail, there is always a great rush of wind behind me and a pounding of feet, and then here come the three dogs, rushing hell-bent up the trail, scattering magpies and grasshoppers. At each intersection, they sit and wait, panting. Then, when I have committed to a direction, they screech off in front of me if they approve of my choice, or give me a surprised look if I have chosen the wrong way around or the way that bypasses the creek.

I'm not used to the prairie, actually. I'm from a land of tall trees and shoulder-level fogs that leave a fairly narrow band of sky. Out here in Wyoming, we are in the middle of ten thousand uninhabited acres. Hogbacks and rimrock break up the horizon here and there, but basically, it's all sky, and you can tell it's a lot of sky, because you can see different weather in different directions—a couple of states' worth of weather. With so much sky, there's no lingering for the sun; it's got to keep moving or it won't make it across on time. So, it is either night or it is day, the sun blasting up over a dark ridge, and suddenly it's hot. Or, you just get comfortable with a glass of wine, waiting for the sunset, shading your eyes, and bam, a few clouds in the east turn pink and it's night. There's nobody out here but Frank and me, and for the last two weeks, there's been nobody out here but me, because Frank went to Germany for a meeting.

So now I have four reasons not to like dogs. Four. They make me lonely. I don't know what to say to a dog. "So, how was your day?" I venture. "Roll in anything disgusting?" This conversation the dogs find fascinating. They edge closer and lift their noses, as if they think they could understand English if they could just smell it better. If I ask a question that involves higher-order thinking skills—"So. Do roadkill deer taste better than raccoons?"—they whine and wag their tails. But they don't answer. They never tell me what injustices they suffered at work, or how they fixed the car.

Talking to a dog makes you feel like you're the only person in the universe. "And what would that be like," I ask the dalmatian, "if I were the only human being under this entire sky?" Wrinkles appear on Duke's spotted forehead. "For all I know, there could have been some plague, and I could be the only person left on this planet." Tails bang back and forth on wooden planks. I reach out and scratch a floppy ear. After a while, I give up trying to make conversation and sit on the steps. The dogs settle down, leaning on me, sitting on my feet, resting their chins on my lap. I put an arm around Spike's shoulders, and we all watch the sun drop into night, plop, like a quarter in a slot machine.

FIELD NOTES FOR
AN AESTHETIC *of* STORMS

Frank rolled down the window and shouted over hammering rain to a man who was lifting a chain saw from the bed of a pickup truck. "Any chance of getting through?" Rain drove in the open window, wetting our laps and filling the car with the smell of crushed bracken ferns and pines. A shattered Douglas-fir blocked the road, lying full length where it had fallen in a litter of cones and needles, taking out a three-strand barbed-wire fence. A cow picked its way through the tangle of wire, clambered up the bank, and stood dumbfounded on the pavement, rain eroding the mud on its flank, wind catching at its tail.

"Easy, easy," the man said, but he was talking to his cow. He reached into the pickup and pulled out a can of gas. The cow swung its head from side to side as if to survey the possibilities, then turned abruptly and swayed down the road. The man jerked the cord on his chain saw. Exhaust fumes sank under the weight of the rain as he pulled the chain smoothly through a limb.

I turned back to the maps while Frank jockeyed the car around. We had tried to approach the coastal forest from the north, but downed trees and power lines blocked that road at the river. We circled down the coast and tried the Beaver Creek road, but that was impassable too: bridge out. Everywhere, we had come up against shattered stumps and limb-littered highways where trucks flashed yellow warnings that blinked in the water drops on our windshield. My map showed one more possibility. So we turned south on Highway 101, dodged around sawhorses blockading a parking area, and finally came to a trail that descended through ancient Sitka spruce to a saltwater cove.

Gale winds were plowing through the crowns of the trees, dragging clouds and sheets of rain, making a tremendous noise, but on the forest floor a hundred feet below, the air was still and saturated. Water sifted through spruce needles, collected in the old-man's-beard, glistened on the spikes of sphagnum moss. Before long, my mittens hung low off my hands, dripping as if they'd sprung a leak, and my long underwear stuck to my legs. We climbed down the raw bank of a creek, where flash floods had torn out a section of trail. Sword ferns dangled over the cliff, holding on with a few black threads. Enormous cedars, unimaginably old, had toppled into the creek and shattered, broken ends splintered into daggers of raw wood, branches embedded deep in the duff, upended roots clawing twenty feet in the air. "Oh deathly quiet pandemonium," Nietzsche would have called it, this stillness under the chaos.

The smell was overwhelming. It filled the gully to the brim. Heavy, dense, sweet—never has air been so sweet—it was the smell of cedars netted with the roots of sorrel, the piney dark smell of old stone churches at Christmastime. Rain pants shushing, one leg against another, we walked along as well as we could, climbing over fallen trees or crawling under on our hands and knees. When we came in sight of the steep sandbank where the forest gave way to the beach, a limb arced past our heads and shattered across the trail.

I have sought out storms all my life, without thinking much about why. Long before we knew better, my sisters and I played with lightning on the crest of the Rocky Mountains, reaching our hands toward rocks. The closer we came, the more furiously the rocks buzzed with electricity. We skipped and spun mindlessly in the electric charges, creating music with our bodies, the way children dance in fountains and make music with splashing light. Certainly this was stupid, but it was also irresistible. "Consider bold, overhanging and, as it were, threatening rocks, thunderclouds piling up in the sky and moving about accompanied by lightning and thunderclaps," Immanuel Kant wrote in 1790, ". . . hurricanes with all the devastation they leave behind, the boundless ocean heaved up . . . The sight of them becomes all the more attractive the more fearful it is. . . ." What reed in the human spirit vibrates with the violence of storms?

Sprinting the last few yards of forest trail, Frank and I slid down the bank to the beach. Surf had beaten the salt water into heaps of foam. Frank waded into the slosh and stood looking out to sea while foam surged around his boots. I kicked through the windrows, lifting clots of foam into the wind and sending them sailing across the strand, so that the beach became the sky and I jumped over the clouds. When I opened my mouth to laugh, I choked on wind-driven rain.

For seven days, it has been raining hard in the inland valley where I live. In the mornings, I have to turn on lamps to read the paper in the blue light under a Pacific storm. Rakes scrape the pavement as neighbors drag leaves out of the puddles and pile them in a sodden heap for the city to collect. Big pincer-bearing tractors like stag beetles move down the street to scoop up leaves. In the evenings, we walk downtown to watch the river rise.

When I went out the back door on the morning of the second day, I discovered that a row of hundred-foot cedars had fallen across my neighbor's fence, knocking their garage on its side, taking down the electric lines, and smashing the pickup in their driveway. I stood barefooted on the wet sidewalk, holding the skirt of my bathrobe against the wind, and looked at the blank space where the trees had been. Our children played under those trees through long summers of lean-tos and jungle campaigns. In the darkness behind the hedges, they looked for danger and found it: elephant traps dug into the duff and covered with cedar branches so artfully woven that if a father walked through, *la de da, la de da,* he would drop a leg up to the knee and fall on his face. In a secret place behind the camellias, they hid explosives made from match heads and spears made by sharpening sticks against rough sidewalks. Again and again, they tiptoed to the edge of danger, touched it, and ran away.

I went back into the house and started making meatball soup for the neighbors. I know it sounds silly, but what else can you do? Then it occurred to me that I should examine my motives; sadness is a sacred space, and maybe the neighbors would rather not open their door to a pot of meatballs offered like a ticket to a sideshow.

The British philosopher Edmund Burke was convinced that "we have a degree of delight, and that no small one, in the real misfortunes and pains of others. . . . " Aristotle agreed: Why else do people line up to watch tragedy, he asked, and sit enraptured on the edge of stone benches while characters are destroyed? But I found myself protesting as I stood in the kitchen with hamburger on my hands. There is no pleasure in a friend's pain. Something about storms themselves makes me want to get closer; the attraction is wilder than human sorrow. At least two things are going on in any tragedy, and how does Aristotle know which one the audience pays to see? There's the destruction of a human being. But there's also the horrific, unstoppable, slow-motion slide of fate, as fascinating and as beautiful as an avalanche.

And then, on the morning of the third day, the phone rang. A student from my Justice seminar had been asleep in her basement apartment when water from the creek began to flow down the steps and across the floor. Trying not to awaken her, her husband stuffed towels under the door and began piling belongings on the top shelves. Creek water popped out the towels, and when the student got out of bed, she stepped into water ankle deep. Then water in the drains started to rise, overflowing the sink. Brown liquid geysered out of the toilet. Water lifted the bookcases and dumped the books. It upended kitchen cabinets and pried open the doors. It ran madly from room to room, overturning tables, knocking down the sewing machine, opening boxes and dumping the contents, stirring books together with boxes of crackers and open tins of tea, floating the pillows into the bathroom where they sloshed in a back eddy of sludge.

By the time I got there, the water had gathered together in a low place, leaving six inches of sludge that buried everything they owned. We stood on the top step in irrigation boots, cowed by the silence. There, down a flight of steps, was the formless chaos that is the mixing of all things, primordial soup. With hands encased in rubber gloves, we reached into the mud, never knowing what we would pull out. A computer disk. A green sweater. Aristotle's *Poetics*. A tiny pair of patent-leather shoes and a baby's crocheted bonnet, carefully saved for twenty-one years. Herodotus and Freud. A loaf of white bread, now brown and soggy, leaking out the torn end of a plastic bag. The same storm that created such wild beauty on the coast tore up lives inland, and left only sadness and stench.

Three thousand miles to the south, floodwaters loosened the mountainsides in Central America and buried people in their villages and sweet-potato plots—unimaginable thousands of people. Photographs in the newspaper showed glorious clouds reaching to the heavens, and beneath them, brown earth sprouting automobiles and bringing forth shattered window frames. "Born in clouds worthy of Michelangelo," the newspaper said, "the rains in Central America have killed more than 10,000."

There is much here that needs to be explained—beauty and horror in the same sentence. The line between creation and destruction is a fine one, and I should not be surprised to find joy so close to fear.

It's possible that the thrill of storms is only relief—fear transformed into rejoicing by the vision of what happened to someone else and not to you, the laughter that fills the hollow space when fear and horror drain away. Kant said that "the sight of [a storm] becomes all the more attractive the more fearful it is . . . ," but then he added the subordinate clause that changes everything: ". . . provided we are in a safe place." The exultation one feels in storms may be a kind of thanksgiving still to be alive, still to be healthy, to have a home.

I know this feeling, of being safe in a storm. In my life, it's as close as I come to pure joy to wake in the dark and hear a silence so intense it has to mean snow—deep, suffocating snow—and then the sound of a car driving by, its chains slowly chinking down the street. I remember waking as a child to the sound of fathers shovelling snow. It was always the fathers, in nylon quilted parkas and embarrassing, sheep-shorn caps, staying home from work on a snowy day. There would be ice on the bottoms of the windowpanes, and the hardwood floor would be cold under our feet. But my sisters and I had fuzzy misshapen slippers with duck heads wobbling on the toes, and the kitchen table would be set for breakfast, each little triangle of grapefruit flesh cut away from the membranes, a box of cereal and a bottle of milk in the center of the table. Our mother would be at the stove, humming "God Save the Queen," heating butter, cracking eggs. No one was going anywhere. The day was bright with white reflected light.

So I know this kind of happiness. But the thrill of a storm is something different: It doesn't purr, it crackles. I asked Frank if he thought the excitement might be physiological. He studies chemicals in the brain, so he might know. Maybe it's the sudden drop in air pressure, I suggested. Released from the weight of the atmosphere, all your cells expand and lift and your spirits lighten. You have to breathe harder to get enough oxygen, and nothing seems quite fastened down. You tip over a little, like astronauts in training suits filled with air. Like boiling water on a mountaintop, it doesn't take so much heat to get you going. Frank gave me a look that could be called dubious.

"I'm not alone in this," I said in my own defense. "Ask people. Ask them to describe a storm they've experienced from a safe haven." When winds have blown out the electricity, people sit close together and offer up their best storm stories, like campers throwing pine cones in a fire. Everyone has a story. A storm in Paris, Guadalupe, Antarctica, Missouri. A thunderstorm, a hailstorm, a sandstorm, or in Oregon, the ice storm we call a "silver thaw." People speak with the joy and excitement they usually reserve for stories about the births of their children. There is glory in wind, wild beauty in storms, excitement that few other events can provide. Storms drive straight to the emotional center. "You should look for storm receptors in the brain," I told Frank.

Maybe I should try to get Frank to read Aristotle, because when Aristotle talks about the attraction of tragedy, he sounds a lot like a scientist. As destiny closes in on the tragic hero and he falls to his knees, tearing in a frenzy at his eyes, waves of pity and fear rise up in the audience, engulf them, and then—this is the important part—ebb away. Tragedy purges people of strong emotion, the way some medicines are said to purge bodies of evil humors, and their souls are lightened and delighted. "To purge the mind of those and such-like passions," Milton wrote, "is to temper or reduce them to just measure with a kind of delight."

So is my pleasure at storms a purgation, an emptying, the analog of pus? I try to be open to this idea, but honestly, I suspect that the opposite is true. Maybe the value of Greek tragedy is not in the ebbing of the tide of sorrow and horror, but in the height of the waves of emotion, the peaks and troughs.

On the other hand, it might be that storms are beautiful. Simply that.

All the elements of beauty can be found in the way light strikes a wheat field under purple thunderheads: clarity and lucidity, a kind of shine and smoothness, unity and diversity, a formal ordering. So I would be convinced that the attraction of storms is the passion caused by beauty, except for one thing. Beauty, as Edmund Burke pointed out, relaxes. Or if it doesn't exactly relax a person, it arouses joy and cheerfulness. "The head reclines something on one side; the eye-lids are more closed than usual, and the eyes roll gently . . . ; the mouth is a little opened, and the breath drawn slowly, with now and then a low sigh: . . . all this is accompanied with an inward sense of melting and languor." Burke's description of scenic delight warns me that he may not be someone I would want to hike with. All the same, I'll grant him the premise that beauty generally causes a feeling of relaxed pleasure.

But when I pull up a memory of a storm and examine the experience like a specimen, I look in vain for relaxed pleasure, let alone an "inward sense of melting." Here are black clouds pouring over the ridge so fast that before Frank can reel in his fly, the winds have smashed into the river, driving tumbleweeds ahead of them like frightened calves. Dust rips up the bank and spirals through a wheat field, sucking bright straw into clouds that have turned green. Here are our children bent into the wind, holding their collars over their faces, running hard ahead of lightning bolts striking at the pines in the mountains. Single pines disappear in a puff of steam, then burst into flame. A tent snaps back and forth, pulling at its stakes. I lunge for it, but it lifts off the beach, rolls through the campfire, and cartwheels across the river, scattering flames like a St. Catherine's wheel. Grabbing as much gear as we can snatch from the wind, we dive into the other tent. All the rest of that day and into the night, we lie tangled together, wiggling and whining like a pile of puppies, while rain pours down the seams of the tent and wind lunges through the darkness, slapping the tent flat. Each time the tent recoils, water snaps off the fabric and rains onto our faces.

So now. Was the storm beautiful? Yes, when it was far away. But the inside of the storm was horrid: "dark, uncertain, confused," Burke said. And it wasn't calm I felt in the middle of that storm, but a heightened excitement, a close focus, an intensity close to fear—the very opposite of beauty. But move carefully here, Burke warned. The opposite of "beauty" is not "ugliness." The opposite of "beauty" is "sublimity," the blow-to-the-gut awareness of chaotic forces unleashed and uncontrolled, the terror—and finally the awe. To experience the sublime is to understand, with an insight so fierce and sudden it makes you duck, that there is power and possibility in the universe greater than anyone can imagine. The sublime blows out the boundaries of human experience. Is this, finally, what we crave?

Storms are our wilderness. A few generations ago, people looked to wild lands for the experience of the sublime. In thick slabs of yellow and violet, Albert Bierstadt painted light that threw the Rocky Mountains into terrible shadow, and even in the cities, people knew there was omnipotence in the advancing clouds and infinite time in the depths of rock. But now we tidy up the wild places and manage the mountains for scenic pleasure. Scientific explanations make nature plain. Highway systems make it easy. Where I live, I can stand on the top of Marys Peak and look west across land that once stopped settlers in their tracks. There were endless forests blockaded by rhododendrons that pioneers called "mountain evil," and salal and burnt snags so thick that they could not be penetrated. That same landscape is merely beautiful now— the orchards, the lichens in the hedgerows.

But in one of those ironies that mock human purposefulness, the harder people try to control wilderness—draining wetlands, burning forests, clearing mountainsides, paving meadows—the wilder the weather becomes. If people are looking for wilderness now, all they need to do is turn their faces to the sky.

Philosophers have a phrase that might describe this celestial wildness. It's an awkward tumble of clauses that they use as a definition of god—"that greater than which nothing can be conceived." Our ancestors spoke to storms with magical words, prayed to them, cursed them, and danced for them, dancing to the very edge of what is alien and powerful—the cold power of ocean currents, chaotic winds beyond control and understanding. We may have lost the dances, but we carry with us a need to approach the power of the universe, if only to touch it and race away.

THE WESTERN SINGING FISH

The first cut scrapes through hard sand that falls off the shovel with the shape of the blade still on it. The second push cuts into mud and clicks against pebbles and the rough edges of oyster shells. The hole fills with water, and the third shovelful flows off both sides of the blade, leaving clams scattered on the flat. I kneel down to pick them up and drop them, clanking, into the bucket.

The clam flats lie broad and bare, a mile from the base of the Olympic foothills to the blue line of the bay. Out here in clean air, people look as though they're floating a few inches above the sand—a couple of teenagers carrying buckets, a woman with a picnic basket, two men leaning over a rake. A woman holds a dog on a leash while she laughs with her daughter; when the dog walks around them and then pulls away, they spin together like dancers, unwinding. Sandpipers run in packs along the waterline, whistling sharply, and a few western gulls circle over a fishing boat at anchor on the sound. I can hear their food calls from here—loud, piercing, linear cries that can be heard over slapping waves, cries that can carry on a gale, cries as clear and sharp as salt air.

My son and I are in charge of gathering oysters for dinner, so as the tide falls we set aside our clam shovels and walk among the rocks, prying open oyster shells with blunt knives and dropping the oysters into a plastic bag. It's the lowest tide of July, and the beach is paved with oysters bleached white under the blue expanse of sky, oysters clinging to every rock, to each other, layer on layer, sharp to walk on. But this is work that cuts your hands, and what's under the stones interests us most, and soon enough we have set the task aside and we're lifting rocks. There are unexpected worlds under the rocks along a coastline—shore crabs thick as cobblestones, periwinkles, and bright green isopods. Jonathan turns over one slab of rock and there, stuck to the underside, are hundreds of orange eggs. Some of the eggs have hatched into silver fish that stick to the rock with suction cups, flank to flank, like sardines in a can. Jonathan reaches into the puddle under the rock and gropes around in the silt. He brings up a squat and ugly fish that flaps in his grip. The fish is humming.

It isn't exactly singing a tune, but the fish is distinctly humming, a buzz so deep and rough it's almost a growl. I have never heard this sound before, but I've heard of the fish. It must be the toadfish some people call the western singing fish. When the time is ripe, a male toadfish hollows out a nest in the sand under a rock ledge and then hunkers down, humming a one-note song. If you stand quietly at the edge of water at night, I've been told, sometimes you can hear the fishes humming in the dark—maybe just one, but maybe several, the different pitches rising off the water to make a deep droning chord that goes on and on all night. The sound draws females who swim through the dark toward the music. They slip into the hollow, roll on their backs to lay their eggs on the bottom of the rock, and slide out again before dawn, leaving the males to guard the nest.

I can see my son mulling this over, and I'm curious too, wondering what lust is like for a fish. What sensation runs down a female's flank when she hears—or does she feel—a fish song from away down the dark beach, drawing her like gravity? What does it feel like to be sucked toward a song? With what trembling joy, what unbearable vibrating anticipation, does the male hide under the rock, humming his damp love song in the dark?

My father could hum and whistle at the same time. He mostly did chords, and sometimes sequences of chords, but he had a few songs worked up, "Aura Lee" and "Tell Me Why," an old love song he whistled to my mother. This seemed to be a worthwhile talent to cultivate, and I practiced long hours, but I can't claim much success. When I try to hum and whistle at the same time, the tones that emerge in the humming and in the whistling don't match up, and the whistle always wins out in the end—*as the blackbird in the spring*—while the humming drones along behind.

It doesn't surprise me that the whistles win. There is urgency in the line of a song, a pressure to go somewhere, to get on with it, to be done. The composer Robert Schumann was very fond of naps, but when his wife wanted to wake him up, all she had to do was go to the piano and play an unfinished scale. *Do re mi fa sol la ti.* Soon enough, Robert would shuffle downstairs in silk slippers, cross to the piano, angrily punch *do,* and go back upstairs to get dressed.

We feel compelled to finish the scale, to go the distance. The alarm call of the telephone attracts our attention, and what goes unheard is the deep humming of the universe, of roots pushing through soil, of warm air circling the equator, of creatures breathing in the sand, and tides rising and falling. Over the soft, repeated rhythms of the tide, human time marches loudly on and we step lively to the music.

Time moves in a line, Saint Augustine said sixteen hundred years ago. God took that time line and chopped it up, giving a little piece to each person. So I skid down my little allotted segment of the time line, my hair blowing back in the wind, my shirt pressed against my chest, my arms and legs pinwheeling, my eyes squeezed shut. Sometimes I feel myself screaming, but Frank wakes me up and laughs at the little "eep, eep" sounds I have been making, and we go outside together and look at the stars.

One evening many years ago, when we were walking in Athens, Frank and I came to a cyclone fence encircling an entire city block that was excavated twenty feet into the ground. There were students in the hole, in the low light and rising heat, gathered around card tables heaped with fragments of marble, or digging with spades. A sign on the fence said that in this very spot, in what had been a marketplace in ancient Greece, the philosopher Zeno explained why it was a mistake to think of time as a straight line that can be divided. If a given distance is infinitely divisible, he said, then anyone who wants to travel that length will first have to traverse half its distance. Because you can't get anywhere without first getting halfway there, and because you can't get halfway *there* without going halfway to that point, and so on and so on, nobody can get anywhere at all. And—this is the good part—the same must be true of time: To pass from one time to the next time, you would have to pass through an infinitude of smaller and smaller pieces of time, and that would take forever.

My friend who is a philosopher says that what Zeno makes her think is, Who cares if you get somewhere? Try instead to go infinitely deep into any piece of the distance. If there is eternal life, she says, it will not be in the length of your life, but in its depth.

This makes sense to me. I have no doubt that my life has a definite limit, even though I don't know today what its length will be. But I don't think there is any limit to the depth of each moment, and I am going to try to live in a way that plumbs those depths, to live *thickly*, extending the reach of my moment down into the mire of detail and up into the damp and cry-filled air.

I know it won't be easy. If I am going to live thickly, I will need to find a way to get out more often from between my roof and my floor—the top and bottom of my life. I live in a house where hardwood floors, a layer of spiderwebs and acoustical tile, eight feet of damp air, a laundry basket of unmatched socks, a slab of concrete, and a six-inch footer of gravel fence me off from the earth. But if I dug under that, I could find an ancient riverbed of round boulders, and below that, sea animals so old they have turned to stone, floating on a lake of burning rocks.

If I could break through the ceiling plaster, the quarter-inch lath, the two-by-six-inch beams, the plywood attic floor, six feet of cardboard boxes full of things I don't need, insulation four inches thick and a plywood roof stuck full of nails, I might discover a single scrub jay sitting on the gutter. I could hear it scold, and high over its head I might hear spiral nebulae squeal as they spin at five times the speed of sound.

Who knows what I could find behind my mirrors if I could get beyond my flattened self, shiny and two-dimensional, always startled or furtive. Sometimes I catch a glimpse of a laughing self, a self entire, and I look back unbelieving, but by then the image is gone. The flat person returns, looking guilty, because I have places to go and work to do, priorities, household chores, and heaven knows we don't have that kind of time to squander.

Up on the tidal flat, Frank and my brother-in-law are still working a clam rake through the mud. The incoming tide is lapping under their long shadows, touching their shoulders and rippling their heads. These men aren't engineers, but they ought to be, for the pleasure they take in a tool so perfectly suited to its purpose. Frank digs the rake into the sand and pulls it toward him, shaking as he pulls so the sand mixes with water and drains through the wires of the basket. When he lifts the rake, he has a full load of clams and stones and oyster shells trailing swags of green algae. My niece is counting out her clams, unloading them one by one into a pouch her mother has made by spreading out the edge of her T-shirt. Their foreheads almost touch, Carley has grown so tall. My sister kneels by a clam hole, her hair curling in wet air. I walk over to where they are digging, push my shovel into the sand and press it home with my foot. The dog lifts itself stiffly and walks over to sniff at the sand.

At the edge of the bay, my daughter is standing in water up to her ankles. There will be fat clams in Erin's bucket, but she will have collected other treasures too—maybe a stone with a hole through it, the spidery vertebra of a fish, or maybe the purple carapace of a porcelain crab. I lift a shovelful of sand and dig the shovel in again.

My son's gaze is distant over the water, detached, and I wonder what he is thinking about, or maybe who, and what words he is using to tell her the story of this day. He raises his arms and runs his hands through his hair, lifting it into the light. It catches gold just for a second, the way it did when he was tiny and his hair was like caterpillar silk drifting wild and insane above his astonished baby's face.

I reach into the hole, groping for clams. Over the line of the sea, hundreds of gulls circle higher and higher, flapping white, like a dissertation lifted in a hurricane. Calls of birds and the voices of people I love cut across the sand—exultant calls of seeking and finding.

At darkfall, we all troop to the edge of the water, standing shoulder-to-shoulder on the sand, hoping to hear the fish sing. The breeze is warm and piney, sliding out of the forest onto the water, lifting our hair. Far out to sea, a light moves slowly across the night. A small plane drones past. A car door slams somewhere up in the campground. We strain toward the water, listening for the longest time, trying to quiet our own breathing. But we can't separate the song of fish, if we hear it at all, from the knocking of waves against logs, and the buzz of our own excitement, and the panting of the dog.

So we build a driftwood fire and move in close. Wrapped in jackets, we hum to each other the tunes we think we might hum if we were fish and we were lonely. All that humming in the smoke from a cedar fire, in the gathering fog, in the salt-smell of oysters steaming, makes the air thick and welcoming and without limits.

SEPARATION

THE SONG OF THE CANYON WREN

*The love of beauty is a longing for the
homeland of the soul.*—PLOTINUS

The song of the canyon wren is the sound of falling water. Its bright
tones drop off the canyon rim and fall from ledge to ledge a step
at a time, sliding down a pour-off, bouncing onto a sandstone shelf,
then dropping to the next layer of stone and down again—a falling
scale, eight tones, a liquid octave of birdsong in the hard, sun-cut
canyon. I lift my binoculars to search the rocks, but I don't find the
wren, which won't surprise you, since you know wrens.

Sometimes sounds turn me almost inside out with longing.
The song of the canyon wren, the faraway voices of my children,
and the watery sound of cottonwoods—these are on my mind
today. But the sound of rain on sandstone will do it too, water hiss-
ing at the side of the lost sea, and the soft breathing of silver fishes
caught between grains in this shelf of stone.

I hear singing, and I don't know what to do. I want everyone
in the world to hear it. Then I want no one in the world to hear it
but me. Then I want to gather Frank and the children and listen

together. Then what hits me is a flood of sadness, washing the stones out from under my feet and making me stumble.

Does this happen to other people? It isn't just sounds. It can be a smell, or a glimpse of something in the distance. The silhouette of pinyon pines on lavender sunrise sky, or a mountain range under rain clouds, each row of mountains softer and dimmer than the row before, or two black ravens stroking in unison across the red face of a cliff—any of these can hit me a body blow that leaves me gasping. This unnerves me and makes me feel ungrateful. I am blessed by beauty beyond anything I deserve; the gift should make me quiet and glad and at peace, but instead it makes me feel hollow inside. I tell you this, I trust you with this secret, because I think sometimes you feel it too.

At first I thought it was loneliness, and maybe that *is* it. My daughter would love the ravens, I say to myself. Or, if only my son could be here. The beauty is too much for me alone; it opens an empty space that I need to share with someone else, and the absence of the people I love fills me with regret. And maybe it's a vastly deeper loneliness, knowing that even if my daughter were here, or my son, they would never see it the same way. Even Frank, the person closest to me in all the world, sees the land through eyes far different from mine. So I will always be alone in my seeing, fundamentally alone.

Or maybe it's the sadness of unsatisfied greed. I want this for myself, and I want it forever. I am greedy for falling water. Grasping after ravens. Gluttonous, when it comes to cottonwoods. The thought that the sky will dim, that the ravens will land and dive their heads into carrion, that the mountains will disappear into deep night, that the moment—never to be replaced—will be lost to me forever, is more than my greedy little emotional center can support. So maybe this is it: Knowing that the moment cannot be captured and held, I mourn the moment as it passes.

Or maybe what I want is to *be* a raven, to merge with the sunrise, to lose myself in the layers of mountains—but I doubt it. So far as I can tell, water falling through sunshine doesn't feel itself falling, doesn't rejoice at the brightness of the light, doesn't know joy or sorrow. If that's true, then to be one with nature would be a pleasure unfelt, which wouldn't be much of a pleasure at all.

A few hours after sunset, the sky glows above the cliff where the moon will rise. Already spires across the canyon are shining white. Bats career over the water, listening for the echoes of insects. Then the face of the moon rises over the canyon wall and every plane of rock and tumbled stone stands bare and white, outlined by its own moonshadow. I can see Frank in his sleeping bag on the sandstone ledge. A single coyote calls a question and then quiets, listening for an answer. I hear a wood rat scuffing in the dry leaves at the base of the cliff, probably looking for last year's seedpods. A locust in the cottonwood tree suddenly stops buzzing, as if it too is listening. Moonlight has washed most stars out of the sky, leaving only Orion beyond my feet, and the Big Dipper over my head. I lie in my sleeping bag, quiet and alert. What am I listening for?

"Almost everyone is listening for something," Sigurd Olson said. "We may not know exactly what it is we are listening for, but we hunt as instinctively for opportunities and places to listen as sick animals look for healing herbs."

Sometimes I think I'm homesick. Sometimes I think that what happens when the landscape seizes me with such sadness is that the moment reminds me of a home I left generations ago, a beloved place I remember in the deepest recesses of my mind. It might be a landscape on an intellectual plane, a Platonic realm of ideas where perfect truth and perfect beauty become one glorious idea that can't be distinguished from love. Or it might be a clean and windswept place, a real place at the edge of water. Maybe something ancient in my mind seeks meaning in the lay of the land, the way a newborn rejoices in the landscape of a familiar face. Maybe I go to the wilderness, again and again, frantically, desperately, because wild places bring me closer to home.

Possibly you think this is all just words, a story I tell myself on dark nights to keep away a greater darkness. It might be so, but there is this fact: Last week, we made camp in a pocket of sand high among sandstone outcroppings above the desert. In the darkness, as stars flickered and the lights of distant campfires flared and fell away, the kettle on the backpacking stove hissed and whirred. But when I turned off the stove, the whirring didn't end. Frank checked the stove for leaks. Finding nothing, he slowly swept his flashlight toward the source of the sound.

In the spotlight was a pale rattlesnake piled like a rope, its tail buzzing, its head probing the darkness toward us. In the whir of the stove and the whir of the snake, I almost understood something. I came so close, but the recognition fell away after the first startled silence, in the excitement of the snake. In the morning the snake was gone, and there was frost on our sleeping bags. The water in the water bottles had frozen, and the eggs, when Frank cracked them against the frying pan, were as clear and round as glass eyes.

And then there's another place. I'll tell you about it, but you shouldn't expect too much, because it's just an ordinary place. We had walked up a dry creek to a clearing where someone had built a windmill. There was a concrete slab and an open basin of thick, green water. The windmill was an ordinary western windmill, held up on steel struts. I sat next to the tank and leaned against a strut. The wind came up warm at my back and the windmill started to creak and knock. Birds came to drink from the basin, including one Frank thought might be a green-tailed towhee. It ran toward the tank like a chipmunk with its tail in the air, but really, there were lots of birds, walking or flitting or diving toward the water. The air was light and warm and, except for the windmill, silent, and the moment was beautiful and true. That's all I can tell you. But I felt I had been given a sudden glimpse of a place I have never been and can only dimly remember.

THE *p*ROMETHEUS MOTH

I was standing with the doctor in the kitchen of my father's house, leaning against the stove. The handle of the oven door was pressing into my back, and I was staring across the room at the moths and butterflies behind glass, framed and mounted on the kitchen wall. It was full-blown summer, a sweet July morning, the kind of morning when my father would have been sitting in a lawn chair outside, reading the paper, greeting his neighbors, inching the chair across the driveway to keep it in the sun. I was a thousand miles from home, and I missed my children.

"Would you like me to do something?" the doctor asked me. "Is it time?"

This should have been an easy decision. My father and his doctor were longtime friends and intellectual companions. On dark, wintry evenings, they stayed up late, the two scientists, and talked about right and wrong, about life, about death. These were pragmatic, Depression-raised men, problem-solvers. If they were dying in pain, they wanted the dying to be quick, and then everyone could get on to other things. The doctor and I were both sure we knew what my father wanted.

And it clearly was time. My father's body was dying faster than he was. We couldn't roll him over in bed without leaving dents in his thighs. Where the skin on his back was sloughing away, only the sheets bound him together. His lips moved sometimes, but we couldn't make out any words, and his eyes never opened. He breathed in loud whispers, then stopped, then cried out and breathed some more. Sometimes he seemed to sob, and once he squeezed my hand (although I may have imagined that), but there was no question in my mind that he was in pain, and that it was a pain the doctor could not end.

But *I* could. I could say one word. I could say yes, and unless I'd horribly misunderstood the doctor, my father's best friend would give him enough painkillers to kill him. My children and husband would come and I wouldn't be alone, and after a while, I would get to go home. I have never been so lonely in my life. If I said yes, my sisters would land at the airport and I would be there to meet them and we would hug and cry and say how good it was that the pain was over, and how this is what Dad would have wanted, and then we would organize things in the house. We are good organizers. Things for the estate sale. Things for the library. Things for my sisters' families. Things for mine. We would remember to cancel his magazine subscriptions. We wouldn't talk about how he died. His friends would bring casserole dishes, and my aunt would bring a ham, and we would send them off with hugs and some little memento—a brass anchor on a bookend, a

biologist's hand lens, a framed photograph of a monarch butter-
fly laying eggs. There would be lots of hugs.

Years ago, when I visited my father, I used to sit with him in the
morning sun and greet the neighbors. The neighborhood had grown
old along with my father, and the people who passed were lifelong
friends. On doctor's orders, they walked around and around the
block, never getting too far from home, stopping to chat each time
they passed. My old playschool teacher came by each morning—
was she eighty-five this year or eighty-six?—not so much walking, as
falling forward and catching herself each step with a leg swung from
the hip. She's in terrible shape, my father confided, but I could see
that for myself. But she always remembered my name, which is
really something, since most of the people in my hometown know
we're all Dean girls, but can't tell one of us from another, and
which is the one who lives in Oregon?

　She didn't come by on my next visit, but the corner neighbor
stopped to talk. "Had I heard?" she asked cautiously. The playschool teacher was dead. She had died. That's what had happened.
She had died.

　But what had really happened was that she and her husband
had gone down to the river in the city park, carrying a picnic basket and the family quilt. They didn't eat a picnic. Instead, they
spread the quilt on the grassy bank and lay down side by side.
Then he pulled a gun from the picnic basket and shot her in the
head, spattering the playschool teacher's blood across the inter-
secting rings of calico, across the tiny patches of bright fabric from
small children's dresses and the aprons of the elderly aunts who

loved them. Then he shot himself. My father told me this, and he told me he thought they had done the right thing. "How much he must have loved her!" my father said. I looked up smiling to meet his eyes, expecting to see them filled with tears. Instead, his look was hard and sharp and pointed, like an eagle's.

"It should never have happened like that," my sisters and I agreed on the phone. "People should be able to end their lives cleanly, privately, without spoiling the quilt. Their children should have helped them. Doctors should have helped them." In the park, no less: We were shaken by this. Of course they would want to die in a beautiful place, that's surely why they chose the river—but right there, dying where children come to play? Where the creek runs down the shale bank under the big-leaf maple trees? Right there, next to the jewelweed and the bees?

If I say yes, what will my father think? Will he think, *I knew I could trust her to figure out what is right and do it without flinching? She always was my problem-solver, and she came through in the end.* Will he be proud of me? His pride has motivated me all my life. Why should it be different now?

Will he protest? *But I was still alive. I could hear the children coming home from school. I could follow the leafy paths of my thoughts. I was remembering a picnic spread along a fallen log, and my daughter killed me. My own daughter.*

If I say yes, will his feelings be hurt? *In the end, when she was lonely, she killed me to get this over with, so her family would come. That's all she wanted, all she cared about—someone to comfort her. Maybe I should have told her to go home and live her life, and she would have gone, and she wouldn't have needed to kill me.*

If I say no, maybe he'll say, *she could have stopped the pain, and she didn't. The last betrayal: My own daughter did not stop the pain.* If I say no, maybe he'll say, *she loved me, but she was afraid.* Will he understand? *Well, it's got to be hard. I can absorb the pain she couldn't bear—what else are fathers for?*

Sometimes, these last years, my father would call me on the phone and leave a message on my machine. He would be crying from the pain, and he would say I should come and help him. I'm standing in my office holding a sheaf of student exams, and my machine is crying. I frantically press the buttons on the phone and the doctor says, "I know, I was there when he placed the call, I can't stop bone-cancer pain without killing him, I wanted to tell you that." I would call my father back and he would be asleep, and I wouldn't come, and I wouldn't help him.

All our lives, when my sisters and I have had a problem we couldn't solve, we have taken it to my father. I remember one night when my sister was working late to finish up an insect collection for her science assignment. She had collected at least fifty insects—ants and bees and butterflies and even a bombardier beetle—and put them in glass jars with carbon tetrachloride. Then she shook them out of the jars and mounted them on long, black pins. One big Prometheus moth would not be killed. While she held it by the abdomen and tried to skewer it to the board, it fluttered and flinched. She poked and missed, poked again, got a new grip on the moth. Sobbing, she tried again and again to stick it through without tearing the beautiful brown eyes on its soft wings. I ran to get my father. He came down the stairs, saw at once the situation, put the moth back in the jar, gave it a walloping dose of carbon tet, hugged my sister, pulled out the moth, and stuck it to the board. It quivered in place, the eyes on its wings wide in astonishment.

I've got to think harder and better now than I've ever thought in my life. I should try to list the pros and cons in two columns and weigh them out, the way he taught me, but I can't make it work. Mercy killing is an enormous act. When I try to weigh out the consequences, the huge fact of it knocks over the careful balance of advantage and disadvantage, scattering the brass weights, sending every other consideration spinning heavily across the floor. It's a Promethean act, dangerous and proud—for better or for worse, stealing fire from the gods. It is beyond ethical categories. It is beyond laws and two signatures and review panels. Nothing requires it. Nothing justifies it. Greater than justice, it is an act of mercy, an act of love. It's a wrong that cannot be forgiven, a sharp-eyed, hard-beaked eagle tearing at Prometheus's immortal liver. It's the greatest gift one person can give another, a gift of stupendous, titanic love.

The silence in the kitchen is starting to congeal, taking on substance that fills the air and seems to glisten. Through the window I can see a neighbor walking by, looking carefully at the house, probably wondering if this is a good time to stop and deciding not. There are robins on the lawn, up to their hips in thick green grass that needs to be mowed. They poke and chirrup, hopping into the air, settling again. I can see the neighbor boy fiddling with the lawn mower in his driveway, getting ready to come over to mow my father's grass, something he has done every week for the past three months. If my father can hear, he will love the sound of a lawn mower starting up and moving back and forth across the lawn, louder and quieter, coming and going. In the end, the sound of the lawn mower is the only thing I know for sure.

"No," I said. "Not today."

TRAVELING THE LOGGING ROAD, COAST RANGE

'm driving between banks of forest duff, through a leafy tunnel lined with sword ferns and foxgloves. Morning fog spreads through the trees and along the narrow road, like milk poured in water. I turn on the windshield wipers and swerve to avoid a salamander. Huckleberry bushes and rhododendrons grow thick under cedars reaching over the road. I'm not sure how tall these trees are; their top branches have disappeared in the fog. I don't know how old the forest is either, but along this road, I have seen scars on the uphill sides of cedars, where Siuslaw people peeled strips of bark more than three hundred years ago. In the undergrowth, in the fog, these are trees without beginning, trees without end: an eternity of forest.

The road has only one lane for most of its length, but every mile or so there's a wider space where a driver can pull over to let a log truck past. There are pink plastic ribbons dangling from branches here and there, and sometimes a mileage number on a plastic post. Thickly paved with asphalt and built to last, the road follows its fogline around the shoulders of mountains and along ridge tops in Oregon's Coast Range. It's surprisingly well built for a one-way road that, as far as I can tell from my topographic map, ends on the top of a hill in the middle of nowhere.

MILEPOST 19

I crest a hill, startle, and hit the brakes. Bare hillside falls away on my left, bare hillside rises sharply to my right, nothing but mud, acres and acres of steep hillside stripped and sodden. A few blackened spars fall across the hill at odd angles, a few more stand upright—each a stake burned to its base. Far up the hillside, a bulldozer is working slowly. I can hear it shifting and wheezing and powering in low gear, gouging into the earth to tear at a root ball, then shoving the broken end of a tree into a pile of slash. A single strand of smoke rises from a smoldering slash pile and spreads out brown against the bottom of the clouds.

I pull off the road onto a landing littered with tree bark. The tracks of heavy equipment have cut the ground into muddy stripes. Through the clear fans of my windshield, everything has been reduced to shades of gray except, far away, the dull orange smudge of the bulldozer. I have seen a landscape like this before, but it takes me a minute to search my memory. It isn't Central America; nothing I have seen in the slash-and-burn agriculture of third-world countries comes close to this kind of devastation, on this scale. Eventually, I pull back to mind a photograph of a scene from Europe—a cloud-shrouded moonscape of burned and broken snags, where even the ground is churned into craters and thrown into pressure waves of mud and slash. In the foreground, a burned-out tank, and below the photograph, the label: "The Forest of Ardennes, 1945."

Fog turns into rain and within minutes gullies are channeling gray water into larger gullies and digging ditches that spill a slurry of mud onto the road. The mud runs under my car, drops off the roadbed, and slides down a ravine toward the river where salmon are pooling up, waiting to move onto spawning beds.

Before I saw the effects of clear-cutting the great Northwest forests, I imagined a romantic picture: Lumberjacks come in and cut down trees, everyone has clean, sharp-smelling lumber for homes and schools, families have jobs and, where there had been a forest, there is a flower-filled meadow, which is nice for the deer and thus for the hunters; and after a time, the forest grows back and the lumberjacks can cut it again. Then I came to Oregon and saw clear-cutting with my own eyes.

Do people know about the bulldozers? Do they know about the fires and the poison sprayed from small planes to kill whatever brush may have survived? Do people know about the steepness of the bare hills and the crumbling edges of eroded ravines, the silt in the spawning beds? Do they know about the absolute, ground-zero devastation? Logging companies don't just cut the trees and haul them away. In clear-cuts I have seen, not only the trees, but the huckleberries, ferns, moss, the fuss of the chickadees, the silver whistle of the varied thrush, even the rich forest duff that holds on to winter rains, the nourishing soil itself, are all gone—hauled off, sawed up, starved out, plowed under, buried, compacted, or burned. All that's left after clear-cutting are steep hillsides of churned-up mud, a few half-burned piles of slash, and a high-quality asphalt road.

MILEPOST 34

On a line drawn as sharply on the landscape as a boundary line on a map, the clear-cut ends and so does the rain. Ahead are steep scrubland hills, steaming in hard light. I pull off the road, pack up my lunch, and push through the brush down a steep grade toward a stream that shows on my map. But after struggling for almost an hour through blackberry canes and nettles, I find myself less than halfway down the hill, stranded on a stump in the middle of a briar patch. I look around cautiously, shading my eyes with my hand. Hot light and harsh shadows make it hard to see. Nothing on this hillside is taller than I am. There are waist-high salmonberry bushes, their stems fuzzy with thorns, Oregon grape as sharp as English holly, and thick tangles of blackberries reaching over everything, like cobwebs.

I jump from the stump onto the root ball of a sword fern and grab for a fir sapling. The fern's roots break free and the whole clump slides ten feet down the slope. I ride it down, landing on my back, my feet out in front of me, one arm wrapped in a blackberry vine that has scraped from my wrist to my shoulder. The hillside buzzes in the sun. I give up on the hike to the stream, and start the climb back to my car.

When I finally push through a last thicket and emerge, hot and wobbly at the top of the slope, I sit down in the only shade on the hillside, shade cast by a wooden sign. The sign reads, TREES: A RENEWABLE RESOURCE. PLANTED IN 1985.

Sure enough, I can see a few young Douglas-fir trees here and there, light green and frothy, about my height. I can also see every alien, invasive, thorned or poisonous plant that ever grew in hot sun on disturbed soil in this part of the country: Himalayan blackberries, Scotch broom, poison oak, tansy ragwort, Russian thistles, nettles. I wonder if people understand that forests don't just grow back. Plants grow all right; plants always grow in Oregon. But what you get is not what you had before—not by a distance, not in a hundred years.

A pickup truck grinds by, slowing as it passes. I wonder what the driver thinks of me, sitting alone in the dirt, glowering at the scrub.

MILEPOST 39

I pull over next to a grove where I can see nothing but Douglas-firs ranging off in all directions. They grow tall, straight and thin, closely spaced, evenly ranked, each almost the diameter of a fence post. For ten feet off the ground, the branches are bare spikes. Then the trees leaf out into a canopy that exhales piney air and a slow drift of dry needles. The forest has the feel of a park—the light dusty and even, the afternoon simple and silent. I walk deeper into the trees, brushing a few needles out of my hair.

I am well out of sight of the road, not thinking much, when the silence finally catches my attention. I stop walking to listen. Where are the chickadees, the bees, the flies? I look behind me. What happened to the hemlocks, the big-leaf maples, the low salal? I take a step backward. Douglas-firs five inches across, everywhere I look. Ten feet apart. Three hundred trees per acre. This isn't a forest. This is a farm. I am trespassing on a fence-post farm. Poisoned and plowed and planted and fertilized as deliberately as a wheat field, this lumber will be harvested as routinely as wheat is cut and threshed. I feel like a grasshopper—nervous, scratching one leg against another, tiptoeing across dusty ground below tall yellow stalks.

It wasn't very long ago that trucks carried one-log loads through my town. Standing in line at the five-and-dime, customers would pass the word. "One-log load goin' by." We would crane our necks and peer past the fabric bolts and Valentine's candy, through the dusty window and, sure enough, a truck would rumble past carrying a section of log so massive, it was all the truck could haul on a single load. I try to remember now what I thought then, and it seems to me that I felt admiration for the log, but had no understanding that in the place where the tree had grown, another like it would not grow in my lifetime, nor my children's, nor my grandchildren's . . . not in fifteen generations.

The five-and-dime is a used-book store now, and the trucks that come by carry thirty, forty logs a load—thin logs, destined for pulp or fence posts. Logs hang out the back and flap up and down whenever the truck hits a bump in the road.

MILEPOST 46

The road climbs in a spiral around a bare mountain and finally ends at the top of the hill in a broad expanse of gravel. I get out of my car to look around. I'm guessing that a high-line used to work about where I am standing. Although the hill has grown up in brambles, the earth still bears the marks of skid trails where cables pulled logs up the hill to the yard. This high up, I can see all the way to the afternoon sun and the white line that marks the ocean. From the top of the range to the edge of the sea, the landscape is a patchwork of clear-cuts, replants, landings, bare earth, and a few reserves of old-growth cedar and hemlock along the coast.

When I walk to the far edge of the hill, I learn that I am not alone up here. A man sits in the cab of an old pickup truck, staring out over the fading hills, never looking my way. The hair on the back of his neck is gray and curling, the skin moist and brown from the sun. He wears a plaid shirt covered with a quilted vest and his hands, still gripping the steering wheel, are enormous.

What does he hear, listening so intently? Faint on an old wind, the creak of cables maybe, the shriek of the whistle-pig, shouted commands, men calling out, chain saws shaking with power. Trucks gearing up, logs thudding onto huge log-decks, and the cracking, cracking, as a tree falls through the forest, breaking off limbs, rending the long fibers of its trunk, then silence—a long, terrible silence —and a great thud as the tree drives its limbs into the earth, rises once, settles. Faint on an old wind, the smells of lubricating oil, diesel exhaust, coffee, dust, and the sweetness of new-cut cedar, as beautiful as Christmas.

A few patches of forest are left on old homesteads and in locked-up forest reserves on federal land. A few more plots to cut, a couple of lawsuits pending that may release some logs, some salvage logging after burns in the Siskiyous and Cascades. Three years maybe. Maybe four. Then the logging companies will pull up stakes and look for somewhere else to cut. His children will leave then, too; there's no work for timber workers where there's no timber. One son off to the fish-packing plants in Alaska maybe.

Another to California. Once the daughter with the new baby leaves—for Portland? Spokane?—what will he hold in those great rough hands?

Both he and I can see clear to the sea. The view from the end of the road is a landscape of irretrievable loss.

CAST YOUR *f*ROG ON THE WATER

"How will I know?" Jonathan mumbles. He flops on his stomach in his sleeping bag, still sound asleep. I prop myself on an elbow and stare at him, waiting for another question to surface. It's a black night, full of stars. The Big Dipper hangs handle-down behind Jonathan, drawing a question mark that seems to emerge from his head, as if he were a cartoon.

"How will you know *what?*" I ask, thinking I might lure his subconscious into conversation. Damp air drifts past, carrying the smell of the silent lake, of tule marshes, of silvery fish moving along the gravel bottoms. "How will you know when your flight leaves? How will you know what classes to take?" Silence. I take another tack. "How will you know where fish are holding? How will you know when to set the hook?" We lie on stone that was fluid not too many thousands of years ago. The rocks around our campsite undulate and swirl like water, flow back into eddies, tear loose and pour into the ravine, crack, break, tumble into rough piles and ledges. "How will you know the meaning of life?" That's a stab in the dark, but what's to lose? Jonathan sleeps peacefully, curled in his sleeping bag with only a fan of blonde hair showing under the flannel, and I lie awake, my mind rummaging for an answer to a question I haven't figured out.

At the head of the cove where Jon and I are camped, water from the lake flows into a crack in the basalt and drains down a hole, glugging and thumping like beer emptying from a bottle turned upside down. I don't know where the water goes next, but there's a good strong current going down that hole, pulling along underwater algae, carrying the round seeds of water lilies and a scattering of pine needles that drift from trees rimming the lake. The way I imagine it, the lake must flow into a lava tube and move steadily downward through a tunnel of rough broken stone—an underground stream pouring through darkness, bursting above ground, then diving back into the earth. I listen to the glug, glug of the draining lake and wonder what to say to my son in the morning. *Check the flight departure display. Talk to your adviser. Your father would tell you to look for fish where the current touches still water. Set the hook as soon as you feel a tug; if you hesitate, it's gone.*

A light wind picks up a corner of the tarp and lays it down again. I think I hear a sound like movement in a plastic bag. I chide myself for not hanging the food out of the reach of mice. I wonder if there are bears.

The lake we're camping on is clear and icy cold. When we floated over the main channel this evening, we looked down and saw the lake bottom as clearly as if we were looking through winter air. The water held great green cumulus clouds of algae and, where the current was stronger, cirrus nimbus and green horsetail clouds. On top of the underwater sky floated a reflection of the sky above—layers of truth, and among them swam the brook trout, as long as the distance from my fingertips to my elbow and bigger around than I could span with two hands. Their slightest movements sent light rays darting against the channel floor. When I looked away, the trout disappeared, leaving only their shadows. It was tough fishing, with the water this clear. Jonathan cast a speckled-wing dun again and again into the gathering darkness.

When you're floating on water in the dark, you realize with a certain uneasiness that you have to take a lot of things on faith, but how is that different from the day, after all? I have boated on water so clear that for all I knew, there was no lake and the canoe floated suspended in air. I have walked beside water so littered with dried leaves and broken twigs that it might have been the forest floor, but when I stepped onto the carpet of leaves, I sank into water over my head. I once read about a physics professor who took atomic theories to heart, who truly believed that what looked like solid matter was in actual fact empty space in which a few charges of negative energy spun around a few charges of positive energy. He huddled in the corner of his office, afraid to walk across the floor for fear he would plunge into the atomic abyss. Once, in Ohio, I stepped onto a layer of ice that slowly sank below me until it rested on the lake floor and I stood knee deep in icy water. You can't know, I guess, until you give it a try.

A fish rose to the surface of the lake; we saw only the bulge of water over its back. Rings grew from the point of contact and expanded toward the tule marshes—white rings on black water, washing through tules. Young ducks worked the hatch, motoring zigzag across the water, scooping up mayflies, one and then another, except that I don't know this really; what I saw were white V's on black water—shaking, shimmering V's of light trailing after spots of darkness that I took to be ducks. Spots of darker air shot through the night, hitting the water and leaving a vibration of light, zinging across the canoe, darts of darkness visible against the glowing aluminum, invisible against the water.

How will I know? For twenty years I have studied philosophy and for twenty years I have not cared about the answer to this question. Philosophers fretted that the world would disappear if they turned their backs, but I closed their finely argued books, switched off the light, and it was their worries that disappeared, not the world. But now I have fallen in love and borne children and seen them walk onto airplanes and disappear and then reappear from another airport runway in another place at another time—manifest, hidden, manifest—and when they disappear, the only evidence I have is the sound of their voices, transformed into positive and negative electrical impulses and mechanically reconstructed in my own phone, and now the skeptics' worry captures me and holds me hostage.

"Describe yourself," I say to my daughter across the continent. "Convince me." "Okay," she says, "I am sitting on the edge of a bed that is covered with a piece of fabric from Guatemala. I can see my knees." "On the edge of the bed?" I say. "What else?" "I am holding the phone in one hand and a cup of tea in another. Behind me is a window that reflects me, so I am two people tonight." She laughs, delighted that the evidence confirms a lie. "Behind my reflection is darkness, but in the morning there will be a sugar maple in that place, and a squirrel that jumps around in the branches and never worries about falling." "Never worries?" I say, "How do you know?" She laughs again, too young to care about squirrel-fear, about what would happen to a squirrel suddenly afraid of falling. "I have slippers on my feet and I am wearing my bathrobe, tied shut with a sash." "Tell me more," I say. "Then I'll tell you about a story I am writing," she says. "Ah," I say, "tell me a story I can believe."

Stories are all you have, aren't they, when you get beyond what you can see? You make up theories and if they fit together, you call them true. Philosophers call it the coherence theory of truth, but it's only telling stories, and if all the details are right, if they fit together without contradiction, you believe them. Here is why I believe that my daughter still exists: because the darkness she reports from her apartment fits with what I know about time zones on a map and the turning of the earth, and the bedspread she describes matches the folded fabric I saw in her duffel bag three months ago. I recognize the melody in her voice, and if her voice is thinner than I expect, maybe this makes sense, given what I know about how the telephone works and how she feels tonight. The daughter I remember is consistent with the person who notices a squirrel, who tells a story, who does not think about falling. Sometimes coherence is all you've got, and then it has to be enough.

With a cinch knot, Jonathan tied on a new fly—dangling marabou feathers and a brush of deer hair meticulously clipped to give the impression of a young frog resting on the lake in the dark, its legs hanging, dangerously exposed: a catastrophe tied to a 3X tippet. He flipped it onto the water, where it landed with a splash. He twitched the rod. A white streak shot across the black lake. The rod bent. A flash of white water sprayed into the air. The leader cut a fine line toward the tules. Then up through air, driving toward darkness, a silver shape rose, hung above the lake, then fell heavily on its side. White rings washed into the tules and faded away. The line cut slowly toward the boat. Jonathan lifted his rod and scooped a splash of light into his net. He ran his hand down his line, twisted the fly, and a shadow of a trout flipped its tail and disappeared among the shadows of the underwater clouds.

Believe away, Jonathan. Fish in the dark. Cast your frog on the water.

MEMORY (THE BOATHOUSE)

Snow this morning. A chickadee appears at the feeder, snatches a sunflower seed, flashes its wings and disappears. A pine squirrel crouches on a branch and chatters, its whole body vibrating with distress. The squirrel will cache piles of spruce cones and sunflower seeds that will sustain it through the winter. But the chickadee hides sunflower seeds singly, one tucked in a flap of bark on a white pine, another lodged in the tight place where a branch joins the trunk, another in a crack where a twig has broken off—a thousand seeds cached in a thousand places across its half-mile winter range. When cold weather comes and the easy food runs out, the chickadee can return to each hiding place and find a seed.

The chickadee must have an eager and expansive memory to recall all those hiding places in the complexities of a spruce forest, and a reliable memory, since a chickadee's life will depend on finding enough food each day to survive each winter night. In late fall, as the hidden seeds accumulate through the forest, the memory area of a chickadee's brain—the hippocampus—begins to grow. By early winter, the brain is big enough to hold a treasure map, a complicated diagram of a forest with little X's hanging in the trees. Then, as winter turns hard and the chickadee eats up the seeds, the hippocampus shrinks measurably and becomes a map of a poorer place, a map with shadows at the edges.

I reach for binoculars. The snowflakes are bigger now. Flurries of chickadees drop into the feeder, moving faster than the falling snow, hurrying ahead of winter.

Somewhere in my files I have a map Frank drew me on the day I met him. I finally find it under J—why J, I don't know, but that's close enough to *I*sland, and I am relieved to find it anywhere. The map is sketched on a napkin from the Shack, a shop where students drank coffee when they cut classes. Here is the wavering line of Lake Huron's north shore. Little zigzags and triangles cluster above the line: white pine forests and granite mountains. Eventually, the line wanders east to an X labeled *Espanola* and dives south through *Whitefish Falls* to a set of scribbles where fish shapes tangle like herring in a seine. Then the line picks up again and moves south to a cross in a box, *church,* and turns west to *Birch Island Landing.* Within the curve inscribed by the line, Frank drew scalloping waves: *Bay of Islands.* A flock of dots bobs on the waves. One of the dots is circled. This is the island Frank's family owned when we were young.

Even now, after all these years, I can put my finger on any point along that map and find the memories that live in these places. There are stories in swamps and jokes at intersections, old anger at a truck stop, sleeping children slumped against my shoulder at the

Canadian border, and at Birch Island Landing, memories of hugs that reached precariously from the boat to the dock.

I look back in time and find myself in the driveway of Frank's family home in Ohio on the night of our wedding day. It must be dark because there are lightning bugs. Frank and I are loading the car. I don't remember saying good-bye and it is beginning to seem that I can't remember anything that happens in the dark. The night-clad times have faded away and what remains in my memory are the spaces of light—the interior of the car with the doors open, the fan of light in front of the car, then the light inside the turnpike tollbooth, silhouetting a short-haired woman, then the white forest rotating behind us, as if it were the edge of a record. The next memory I find is the night smell of a gas station in Michigan: motor oil and grass growing. The next morning, we're driving toward a wide horizon in Ontario, an unfamiliar interior that makes a newlywed draw in her breath and wonder what it means to be transplanted into another person's family, a scrubland of stunted pines and heathers and Labrador tea, a land floating on thick mats of sphagnum moss, a real landscape, but not a solid landscape, the way memories are real, without being solid.

Next I'm standing on the dock with Frank, excited to be finally so close to the island. We're watching the whitecaps, deciding that the skiff can handle both weather and luggage. Ojibway children cluster around us, asking questions, helping, tripping on the dock's uneven boards. Now it's evening, a silver salmon sunset and dark sky overhead, and suddenly here's the memory of a long fish dancing on its tail, reaching toward the sky, shaking the hook out of its mouth. It is a huge fish, a muskellunge.

When philosophers search for what makes a person who she is, they come again and again to memory. If I suddenly had a different body, I might still be myself. If I suddenly had new ways of acting and reacting, I might still be myself, although changed in puzzling ways. But if all my memories were replaced by another person's—if, when I searched my memory for my children, they were someone else's children; and when I thought of my high school graduation, it was someone else's past I found—then wouldn't I be that other person?

And if memories define who we are, then does this say something about love? When I share memories with Frank, when the fish that dance in my memory dance also in Frank's mind, don't I become part of him? All those afternoons in the coffee shop when we should have been in class, Frank told me his family stories, and no wonder I began to feel close to these people I had never met. It has to do with X's on a map, memories of the way bog water tucks under the rolled edge of moss on the north end of the island, and the time when Frank's brother dove into the lake after a legendary bass and wrestled it onto the dock.

If love is bound up in memories somehow, and if memories are rooted in places, then love must also have roots in the landscape. I wouldn't swear by the logic of this, but I know what it's like to come to a place and find there, in that place, in the slant of the light or the feel of a floating dock under my feet, the memories that draw me into this family. And I know what it's like to stand at the edge of the lake, looking out together, and feel love so lasting and strong I could swear it is made of granite and wind across water.

So I worry about the shadowy places where memories have disappeared. Frank's parents sold the island when they were no longer healthy enough to feel comfortable alone, so far from the mainland. Now I find myself gathering up the stories, putting them in places I think I can find again, passing the maps along to my children, hurrying ahead of winter.

"Do you remember the boathouse?" I asked Frank's parents. I had called them long-distance from Oregon to check my memories, trying to fill in the blanks, wanting to get the details just right. "I was thinking today about how the boathouse smelled when I opened the door—new pine boards and gasoline for outboard motors, and the bright, green smell of the lake."

"Yes," Frank's father said. "There was a pile of sticks in the corner. An animal."

After a long moment, Frank's mother finished the thought. "It was a beaver."

"Yes, it was a beaver, brought sticks to make a house in the boathouse. There were some other animals . . ." He paused again.

"Mink," she said.

"Yes, mink."

Three people on the telephone line, speaking from three rooms on three phones, all groping into the past, like children holding hands in the dark.

"I remember coming to the boathouse in a storm," I said. "In the wind, the doors rocked in and out, squeaking, and waves rang against the gasoline drum like a bell."

"Yes, we always had a big drum of gasoline and outboard motors clamped to two-by-eights along the wall. The aluminum boat was in there, floating in the slip between the rocks," she said.

"What were those rocks?"

"Granite. Pink granite, the color of grandchildren's cheeks," Frank's mother said, and I could see her again, standing on the granite knob by the flagpole, wearing tailored slacks, elegant even in the wilderness.

There had been a rack of brass hooks on a joist, where fishing poles hung from their tips. I remember how steady Frank's father was, with his surgeon's hands, slipping the topmost guide over a hanger, hardly looking, careful not to laugh at the rest of us who held wobbling poles in two hands and jabbed at the joist.

"The light in the boathouse, do you remember that? The way sunlight splashed up on the rafters on those bright, windy days?" I remember there were minnows, schools of silver minnows under the plank across the slip. We waded in the boathouse and tried to pick them up with our hands.

They slid out of our hands, always. Even when we thought we had one, if we lifted our hands, the minnow was gone. But it doesn't matter because when I think of minnows and Frank's father, I see a tall, broad-shouldered man standing on the dock with sun blowing in his white hair. He reaches into a box and pulls out a handful of oatmeal. Then he picks up a skinned pole that has a square net hanging from four strings. He lowers the net into the water. Then he leans over and tosses the oatmeal into the center. The grandchildren are quiet now, holding their breath as minnows charge the floating oats.

When the net is dark with minnows, Frank's father heaves on the pole and lifts the net from the water. Minnows spill off the edges and water pours out in a heavy rain. In the center of the net, minnows are flapping wildly. He reaches in, scoops up a handful of fish, and puts them in the bucket. Grandchildren dance around him. One drops to her knees to cup her hands over a minnow that has fallen, flicking, on the dock. She tries to scoop it up before it flips back into the lake or wedges in a crack between the boards where she will find it the next day, stiff and dry, and she will pry at it with a stick to pop it out for gulls.

Until someone misplaced them, there were color slides. We would all settle in to watch, sitting on the floor and on the arms of sofas. Here is a bobbing image of a broad deck over granite shoals and a shadowy seagull named Ralph. Then there is a click and a slide drops into place sideways. Men young and old fiddle with the projector. Here the camera looks down a narrow path through a forest of white pine. Click. Blank light floods the screen, painful to look at. They try again. A child sleeping inside the curl of a white German shepherd, and this time two slides drop in at once. The machine jams. Faded images overlap, the forest superimposed on a close-up of what might be a largemouth bass.

We watch a series of faded snapshots, dim and flicking, always disappearing. The grown-ups pretend it doesn't matter, the young people lose interest. Someone fixes another round of drinks. Then this: four smiling children sitting along the edge of the dock, their legs dangling, a white puppy disappearing from the frame. There is pleasure and laughter in these images, but everyone is braced, knowing enough to expect the blank white screen, the futile hum of the projector, the slides jammed. Now here is Frank as a young boy, holding up a pike as tall as he is. His father stands in the background, and if I look closely, I can see that it's his father's arm that supports the weight of the fish. Time has changed the photograph, softening the hard colors, bringing up the shadows.

An artist once told me that if you want to paint a person, you must paint the shadows on his face. Look closely to see the colors in the shaded areas, she said. Shadows are never black. They hold all the colors of the palette—brown and blue and gray, but also orange and yellow, lavender and green. There is pink in shadows sometimes. The colors of the dark places waver and change, so be careful, she had said: Watch them over time. There are textures in shadows, and this is important. Wet darkness shines, but there is dullness in other shadows. Look closely: Does his sweater cast a shadow on his neck? Are there shadows in his eyes? Study the shapes of the shadows, their densities, their curves and angles, because a shadow defines the shape of what it falls on, too.

When a person loses his memories, can we know him by the shadows he casts? What happens to memories when they lose the places where they had put down roots?—the months rearranged, the single disconnected pictures, the places popped off the map. And the other side of the question: What happens to places when their memories move away?—stories gradually bleaching out of granite headlands, meaning dissipating in the steady wash of waves through rushes, and under storm winds, ideas uprooted and tossed willy-nilly on shore. When the landmarks disappear, a white pine forest becomes a tangled slope where seeds transmogrify and shift places, appearing and disappearing, hiding for days and then popping out at unexpected times, a terrifying, scurrying place of dwarfs with perverse senses of humor, and dark caves sealed shut behind magic words no one can remember. Chickadees peck at a flap of bark, bewildered and frightened as the map curls and shrinks. They look around wildly, unable to understand where the memories have gone, wondering if they will last until spring.

A memory from many years ago: We walk down the path to the boathouse. Frank pulls off the hasp and pries open the door. Joists cast leaping lines on the roof. There is deep twilight under the docks, and darting shadows under minnows that school beside the boat. Fishing poles on the rack cast wavering shadows, like bare trees in wind. Turning my head against the acrid smell of old wood and the nests of mice, I cross the boathouse to slide a two-by-four through the framing of the lake-side doors, securing them against wind and ice. A quick look around, then we shut the door and slide home the lock.

BAKING BREAD WITH MY DAUGHTER

n the cabin, my daughter kneaded bread. The dough was thick, unwieldy, and it took all her strength to turn it. When I looked at her, I hardly recognized this woman-child, her face all planes and no softness. She reached across her body to rub her shoulder, leaving flour on her shirt.

This pain has no logic. It makes no sense. There is nothing to be learned from illness in a person so young. The only fact is pain, and the wooden slab of a daughter's face.

"I don't think of it that way," she said. "You can't know in advance if something's good or bad." She turned the bread under her hands and pushed against it with her fists. Fists on dough. A rough, heavy dough: sesame seeds, wheat berries, rye seeds. It will make a good thick nutritious bread. "I've seen people who can't tell the difference between what hurts them and what helps them," she said, "and I don't want to be like that." She turned the bread over on itself, and folded over the folding. The expanding dough resisted

[113]

the turning, pulled away from her fists. The dough had ideas. She pushed it against the side of the bowl. As she kneaded, her face began to relax.

"There is pain that hurts and pain that heals," she said, and I knew she was right. Move even if it hurts, the doctor had told her. With fibromyalgia, this is the way you get well. Healing takes time. Let it hurt, but gently.

Flour and yeast and water. She set the starter on the top shelf of the woodstove and put another log in the firebox. After a time, she added sugar and oil, and more flour, and then all the seeds in the bag. The more she pushed on the dough, folded it over, pressed it with the heels of her hands, the more it rebounded. It's hard for a mother, you know, to see a child bear up. I cried in the kitchen, and then I was ashamed. "What's wrong?" she asked, but the pain in me was the pain in her and she divided the dough into two pieces and shaped it into two loaves.

"What I need from you," she said, "is for you to sprinkle corn-meal on the baking pan." So I did. She took a round loaf in two hands and laid it gently on the pan. Then the other.

The loaves are on the shelf under a tea towel. She can't put them in the oven yet, because we've got the stove too hot. It would harden the loaves before they finish rising. So gently now. Not too much heat. I am trying to learn this. Believe me, I am trying. There will be time for more logs in the firebox. There will be time for an oven heated to 400 degrees. We come away and let it rest. Sometimes patience is as good as hope.

Two egg whites, beaten. Brush them on the risen loaves. Out the kitchen window, there is wind in the birches. Little curls of bark tear away from the trunks and scatter across the patchy snow. The new bark underneath is pure white. Poppy seeds sprinkled on round loaves. Round loaves in the oven, hardening around the edges, still rising in the center. The crust cracks, and steam puffs out the fissures.

Only a few days ago, the birches were noisy with yellow leaves, shuffling in the wind. When we heard leaves blowing across the road, we thought a car was coming; they were that loud. But now the leaves have twisted off the trees and blown onto the lake.

There are fishermen on the bay in their silver boats, leaning over their poles, their hands clasped between their knees; and bear hunters past the portages. We saw them pass today, canoes heavy with gear.

The radio says a cold Arctic air mass is headed into northern Minnesota. There is no color in the sun. Soon we will wake up to a new calm. The lake will be white and shining, with birch leaves frozen in the surface. In heavy coats, my daughter and I will walk on the lake. What will we have learned about winter? What will we know about stillness that we didn't know before?

*P*ALE MORNING DUN
(Ephemerella infrequens)

I usually try to avoid estate sales, the whole of a person's life reduced to things the next of kin don't want, and then priced and spread out on planks. But at eight in the morning, when the line of women with pocketbooks stretches out to the street, I duck through the hedge and come in the back door of my neighbor's house as if I lived here, as if I were bringing soup to someone who is sick.

Inside the house, hazy light drifts from all the windows into the emptied corners, lighting every suspended particle of dust. Exposed to the sun for the first time in twenty years, the walls shine yellow as if they are coated with shellac, but this is tar from the cigarettes Walter and Marnie smoked, shut up in the house with the windows closed to keep out the moisture. The last of Walter's duck paintings are propped against the wall, faded behind dusty glass. In the hall, twenty years' worth of *National Geographic*s

[117]

make two piles as tall as my waist, but every last Louis L'Amour novel has been spirited away.

The bathroom is crowded with shoppers edging around, not touching anything, evidently not finding what they want, whatever that is. All the bottles are open and half empty, and who is going to want bottles that smell of Walter—the sharp smell of sea and cigarettes? Or a tube of toothpaste most recently squeezed on the last day of a man's life? In the open cabinet, a stack of blue towels. A bathroom scale. Woven with gray hair, Walter's hairbrush, like the tortoiseshell reliquary of a saint.

"I know he had a piano," a woman says in an accusatory tone that suggests Walter has somehow taken the piano with him, in utter disregard for her interests. It's true they'd had a piano. The neighbors say that Marnie played it, but we haven't heard music coming from that house since we moved in, which was fifteen years ago.

He'd had guns too, a lot of them. One night Susan, next door, thought she heard footsteps and called Walter. He loaded up a shotgun and crept through her house, threatening the dark space behind each door. Susan, who has dogs and cats and children, followed him around, snapping on lights, saying, "Never mind. Put down the gun. It doesn't matter about burglars." The stuff of neighborhood legend. I wonder who has the guns now.

I push my way through the people who crowd into the kitchen, everybody hurrying to be the first to pick over the good stuff, all complaining because there isn't much left, as if you ever could make anything out of the pieces, as if there is ever anything left after a person dies: a man replacing a washer on the faucet in his backyard, and then pain and darkness (or maybe a wash of light), and then nothing but leftover stuff. There used to be a maple table at the south-facing window where Walter sat after breakfast and smoked a cigarette, watching the street, letting ashes fall into the remains of the fried egg on his plate. The table is gone, but the plates are there on the counter, for twenty-five cents apiece. The big old console TV is still in the living room. How many times had I wanted to throw a brick through that screen when I came to visit Walter and he never turned off the TV, never even turned down the volume. I would take a stab at conversation: "Your roses are beautiful this week." *History for three hundred please.* "Do you like the yellow rose in the new catalog?" *The rationalist philosopher who died of a cold after stuffing a chicken with snow* "I think Marnie would have liked the—" *René Descartes? No, I'm sorry, it was Francis Bacon* "—yellow one with pink on the edges," I said, but Walter said no, Marnie's rule always was, one color to a rose.

Out in the garage, a plank table is piled high with herbicides and pesticides of great variety and potency. Walter raised roses, glorious roses, the most beautiful roses in the neighborhood, roses that towered ten feet in the air and bent under cascades of blossoms drenched with fragrance and color. Horse manure was the secret, he once confided to me, as if I couldn't have guessed—seasoned horse manure and sawdust piled in steaming heaps around the bushes in early spring. All summer, Walter would be out in the sunshine with a big tin bucket full to the brim with poison—Orthene to kill the aphids, Funginex for black spot and mildew and rust, and his special sticker that made the poisons cling to the leaves, even when it rained. Walter had the bucket rigged up to a foot pump and he would be out there pumping, then stopping to breathe, then pumping some more, then breathing, trying to kill the aphids before the pumping killed him. The Queen Elizabeth was his favorite. He had a huge Mr. Lincoln. An Ingrid Bergman. A new variety, Oregold, just put in last year. I look around the garage for his pump system, but don't find it.

A group of men are going through Walter's fishing lures. His rods stand in a corner—spinning rigs mostly, with the line carefully bound to the reel by a thick rubber band cut out of a bike tire. Ten dollars each, but no one is buying. Fishing was Walter's second love, after the roses. He was the one who showed Frank how to rig a single hook with salmon eggs and catch a salmon most every time, even when the other boats were coming up empty. Roses and fishing, and—on special occasions—whiskey. At the neighborhood Christmas party, he showed up in a fresh, hard-starched khaki work shirt and work pants from Sears, an outfit he wore every day I knew him. The fancier the occasion, the heavier the starch. This Christmas, he was so starched up that no one could figure out how he sat down. He sipped Jack Daniels out of the bottle, refraining from smoking in deference to his hostess, who was already mumbling about the whiskey.

Most people's fishing lures get rusty over the years, trolling for coho and chinook in tidewater. Not Walter's. His tackle boxes are as neat as dentists' trays—flatfish, tee-spoons, Heddon spinners, all the lures cleaned up and sprayed with WD-40 and sorted by size. Five dollars a dozen, the estate-sale lady tells the men. Walter liked things clean, and he liked things fixed. The broken wheel on my lawn mower disturbed him. "You know," he told me, watching me mow the lawn while I held up one corner of the mower as well as I could, with twisting pressure on the handle. "You know, most people" (he's speaking very quietly now, looking away), "most people, if something's broken, they fix it." Two more awkward rounds of the front yard and he had that thing out of my hands and apart on his shop bench, and he was rummaging through a box to find a bolt that would hold on the wheel. While he worked, he told me that it was Charlie Russell who learned the secret of how to paint night scenes in the Old West. The trick, he said, is to notice that light at night is pale green, like underwater.

In a corner of the garage are a leaf rake, a shovel, and a couple of anchors that Walter made out of leftover cement poured into milk cartons. There is a sasanqua camellia sapling in a gallon container, ready to be planted. A boat cushion. A set of oars. I wonder where his boat is. He used to keep a little green Jon boat leaned up against the back of his garage. I pick up a lightweight spinning rod that has a Mepps spinner still tied to the line.

I remember the last time Walter had that rod on a river. Frank and I had taken him out on the McKenzie, back in June, a month or so after Marnie died. Light glanced off the riffles and reflected into the new leaves on the cottonwood trees. As the day warmed up, the cottonwoods released the sweet sticky smell that will always mean late spring on a river, and small insects began to show up, here and there, on the water. These were *Ephemerella infrequens,* the pale morning dun. Soon the little mayflies were floating in slow drifts through the eddies, their wings lifted to dry in the sun—a flotilla of tiny sailboats glittering, as if they had ice in their rigging. Some of them had lifted into mating swarms, points of light dancing and swirling, rising, falling, the females dipping to the surface to lay their eggs. Spent mayflies dropped onto the water and floated downstream. All around us, trout rose through green water and nosed into the surface tension, sipping flies.

Frank pulled out his fly rod and tied on a feathery copy of mayfly. He cast downstream and mended his line, letting the current take his fly into an eddy. Walter sat still, as he had sat still all morning—holding his spinning rod across his lap, fingering the line, watching the dancing, dying mayflies, or maybe looking through them to where the river disappeared downstream. Frank lifted his rod and pulled a fish in close to the boat. He scooped it up in the palm of his hand. For a long time, the two men looked at that little trout. Golden in the sunlight, speckled with bronze, chased with silver, it slowly raised and lowered a gill cover that shone as pink as a petal. Then Frank lowered the fish into the river and it was gone.

"Too pretty to keep," Frank had finally said, as if he owed an explanation. As if that explained anything, anyway. As if Walter didn't already understand better than anyone in the boat. Morning always slides into noon. Camellia blossoms, glossy white and heavy on the tree, turn brown on foggy winter nights and pitch on their faces in the driveway. Pale morning duns dance only for a day.

CONNECTION

ON BEING AFRAID OF BEARS

A branch cracks, over by the water. Another branch snaps, closer this time, on the game trail next to the marsh. Is a moose blundering into camp through the dark? A lost canoeist? Or is it a bear, heaving its weight along a trail filled with deadfall? My books say not to be afraid of bears, and so does Frank. Black bears aren't bloodthirsty carnivores, everybody says; they eat like birds—fruits and berries, insects, grass and flowers, young nestlings (if they present themselves), or ants. But I'm skeptical: If bears eat like birds, they must eat like ravens or bald eagles or sharp-shinned hawks, and what comfort is that? If a bear is making its way into camp, reaching with its nose for the smell of food, can it smell us? We tied the food bag ten feet in the air, stringing it up with elaborate care, but then we pitched our tent and laid our meaty carcasses across the trail.

So here I am, enclosed in a tent far out in the wilderness, trying to calculate the size of an animal from the volume of the snap,

[125]

trying to compute the degree of danger from the distance of the sounds. A few pine needles drop onto the tent and slide down the side. A twig falls through a tree, tapping against branches, ticking leaves, landing with a small thump. A mouse scuffs around, the way mice do, but the loudest sound is a noise like a wooden boat creaking against a dock—a sawyer beetle's grub, grinding pine roots into sawdust.

I nudge Frank awake. "If a bear comes, do we chase it away, or do we let it roam around camp?" "Just enjoy it," he says, and goes back to sleep. Irritated, I listen to the sounds of Frank's body breathing, air passing through soft tubes, sloughing over membranes, whispering in and out, like water lapping on stones. Sometimes, when Frank is very quiet at night, the silence wakes me up. Then, unsettled, I roll over and put my head on his chest. Ear to rib, I hear his heart pop and push, blood moving through his veins wetly, like startled fish through reeds.

I press a tiny button on my watch and light shines over the dial. 10:43 P.M. It's starting to get cold. I pull up the zipper on my bag. A frog groans off somewhere toward the water, a sound like sex heard through a motel wall. I'm surprised the cold hasn't silenced the frog, but I'm grateful to hear an animal I don't have to be afraid of. Twigs, for once, have stopped snapping. I lie woodenly, staring in the direction of the side of the tent, as if I could see it in the dark.

"Can animals sleep with their eyes open?" This is the sort of question you can ask Frank.

"Yes," he had said. "Whales do. Mammals that sleep at sea, whales and dolphins and sea otters, sleep with only half their brains at a time. The hemispheres take turns—one standing guard while the other sleeps. So sometimes they sleep with one eye open, the eye connected to the hemisphere on watch."

Look how carefully he explains.

"Fish?" Do fish sleep, glassy-eyed in a rolling, glassy world?

"Yes, fish sleep. At least, they exhibit sleeplike behaviors."

"Do you think that fishes dream?"

Frank hesitated, always the careful scientist. "Probably not. It takes a pretty big brain to dream. Probably when a fish is in a sleep state, there's nothing much going on in its brain at all."

I think of a bluegill floating quietly, dreaming still, silty dreams —nothing but green static with a skim of starshine at the surface. Dark shadows gather beneath the little fish, gauging its size and distance. One shadow separates from the others and rises slowly toward the bluegill. Splashing waves, sound waves, sudden brain waves, a wave of panic. Unable to close its eyes, how does a fish know the difference between awake and asleep, danger and nightmare, outside and inside, light and dark, air and water, reality and appearance? Two universes merge, swirling like water under a canoe paddle, into a vortex that drags into a stream of bubbles and starlight.

A beaver slaps its tail on the water. A raft of ducks kicks across the bay. A gust of wind sets the aspen shaking. Something is down by the shore.

I wish it would go away. I need to sleep. Homeless people, moving from bus-station bench to open doorway, prodded awake by private guards and arriving trains, chronically sleep deprived, become psychotic and can't tell waking from sleeping. What if this happens to me? I tell my feet to relax. Then my legs. Then my hips. But it's hopeless. Before long, all the fibers of my muscles are buzzing under their sheathing. I close one eye and try to hold it shut. 11:45 P.M.

I remember the one night when I could see in the dark. Stabbing around with our flashlights, my friends, Frank, and I had hiked into the wildest part of the sand dunes at the coast. Around midnight, we turned off our lights. The dark was sudden and complete. For all we knew, we stood among sliding black ocean swells, on islands no bigger than our boots. I groped in my pack for a borrowed pair of night-vision goggles and pulled them on. Instantly, a world was created before my eyes, a still, murky landscape in shades of green, like underwater. There, where a moment before had been nothing at all, was an expanse of wavering green sand marked by batches of beach grass, deep in green shadow. The green sand rose in peaks and fell away into green hollows, a rolling oceanic landscape that stretched to the distant green line of pines.

We set off walking. In the dark, without night vision, the others were off balance, stumbling behind me, guided more by sound than by sight, now and then pitching on their faces and picking themselves up, laughing, covered with sand. But with the goggles, I walked along as if it were daylight at the bottom of a shallow sea, picking my way around tufts of grass, scanning the horizon, keeping some distance from my friends who were surely scaring the animals.

"Look," I said. "Coyotes! There, in a line by the forest. Two, three, four of them." I pointed. No response from my friends. I scanned back to them. Frank was looking at me—altogether the wrong direction. "No, over there," I said, and pointed again. He kept staring in my direction. Puzzled, I took off the goggles. Everything went dark. I couldn't see my friends. The coyotes—if they existed at all—had vanished. I couldn't see my feet. I had no idea of direction. The stars were moving more quickly than I thought they should. Suddenly I was afraid that I would fall and spoil the goggles. I put out a foot to brace myself. The soft sand gives beneath me, my legs jerk, and I wake up.

Still night. Still dark. Still all the little forest noises. I pull my sleeping bag around my shoulders. A mouse chews something somewhere near. Grubs grind their teeth. A pinecone falls in the forest. Frank breathes quietly.

"Were the sand dunes really green?" a professor asks, smiling expectantly. I don't know this man, and I don't recognize the classroom.

"No," I say. "They just looked green to me because of the goggles. Dunes are yellow." But as soon as I say this, I know it's no good. Students titter behind me, although when I turn to give them a black look, I see that I am alone in the classroom.

"The dunes just look yellow to me because of the structure of my eye and brain," I admit.

"So what color are dunes?" The professor leans toward me.

"Dunes are no color at all," I say. "Color is in the eye and in the mind."

"So then. What is the sound of a tree falling in an empty forest?"

Is he making fun of me? I imagine a pine silently toppling, bouncing without a sound. It takes down small aspens in its path, and the dry aspen leaves also make no sound, and neither does a nestling bird, tossed out on the ground. After the jangling of the little bones in my ear and the bulging of the tympanum and the firing of the nerves—only then, only there, in my mind, is the thump of a tree on soft earth and the bird's small cry.

The professor moves a step closer. "Color is an idea in your mind, yes. Sound is an idea in your mind, yes. What else?" He is pushing hard. "When you turn off your flashlight, what is left? Turn your back, and the forest is gone. Take off the goggles and there are no dunes. Stop thinking about the bear, and the bear contorts, shrinks, and disappears, like plastic in a flame."

I look around, uneasy. The professor has gone somewhere, although his bicycle is still in the corner. The silent nestling and I seem to be the only ones left. Aspen leaves are falling all around us, golden glints of light spinning down through the dark.

I don't know what makes me open my eyes, but the tent wall is white with moonlight. Through tree trunks, the moon throws stripes across the tent and perfect prints of pine fronds. A tree shadow falls across Frank's face, making him look masked, like Batman. 1 A.M., my watch says. If a bear walked by, I would be able to see its shadow thrown huge against the fabric. If it snarled, I could count its teeth. The wind picks up and the lines of brightness between the trees flicker on the fabric, like rising flames.

Plato says we will never see more than a shadow of the real world. We live as if we were huddled against the dank wall of a cave lit only by a small fire. The fire throws the shadows of the real world flickering against the far wall. This is all we can see: shadows dancing at the back of a cave. We shield our eyes against the firelight, trying to see the details of the shadows, convinced they are real. But even if we see perfectly, it is only shadows that we see. All of us are down in that cave—scientists and poets and shamans. Orange light reflects on our faces and flashes off our ballpoint pens and eagle feathers. We jockey for position, sketching the shadows, crying for more light, more light, throwing wood on the fire. But more light only puts sharper edges on the shadows.

I look out through the mosquito netting to the triangular patch of starlit sky that is all I can see beyond the tent. Cygnus the swan flies straight and true along the river course of the Milky Way, her wings so black they cannot be distinguished from the dark sky. If she keeps her course, the tips of her primary feathers will brush the ears of a black bear hiding in shadow. But if she veers south toward Betelgeuse, she will sail on set wings past the hunter's right shoulder and on toward the great dog—a dangerous neighborhood.

A long low musical tone, like a violin. It lingers and lingers without changing pitch, then fades away. 2:17 A.M. It sounds like the loudspeaker in the JayCees' haunted house, or wind in the eaves. Is it a loon . . . or a solitary wolf?

"Did you hear that?" I nudge Frank awake. "I think it's a wolf," I say.

"It's a loon," he replies, automatically contradicting everything I say, even in his sleep.

The man is a mystery to me. I once asked Frank if he was ever afraid, really afraid. Yes, he said. Once. When he was a child, sick with polio. Just as he was falling asleep, he had heard a small sound like the wings of an owl brushing against his pillow. He lay awake for a long time, his eyes open wide, but the sound didn't come again. As soon as he closed his eyes, though, there it was—soft, feathery, and he could almost feel air against his cheek. Again he lay awake, trying to see, but there was nothing to see, and again, as soon as he closed his eyes, the great wing swept across the pillow. As long as he stayed awake, it didn't come, but when his eyes closed, he could feel its silken touch. Determined to stay awake, he fell asleep with his eyes open, the sleep of the knowing animals.

There's a great crashing in the bushes at the edge of the water. I raise myself up and listen, the skin tight on my head. Frank is suddenly quiet. Branches snap and water sloshes onto the rocks. Then I hear a deep moan. Something big is splashing up the shoreline toward our camp. Crackling branches mark its progress. Whatever it is, it is very, very big. Oh my god. Neither of us moves. The grunt comes again, closer this time. Then we hear a long stream of water drilling into the bay. But the water is drowned out by a tremendous bellow, like nothing I have ever heard before. It is a deep, heaving groan, rising in pitch and volume. It echoes back and forth between the ridges and into the forest. Again, the bellow rolls the length of the bay. What in the world? I'm sitting up and shouting now, and who cares? Nothing can be heard over this noise. I snap on my flashlight. Frank is sitting there with a huge smile on his face, a happiness rare and wonderful. The animal groans once more. Then we can hear it wading out of the water and crashing off down the game trail. Judging from a tremendous crack, it takes a dead pine with it.

Sudden silence returns to the night. Gradually, the forest goes back to its usual noises—chomping, skittering, chewing, rasping. I flop down on my back, and I don't know if the ground is vibrating or if it's my body, trying to get its small parts back under control. I pull my sleeping bag up to my ears and close my eyes, not caring anymore if it's a bear or a moose or kingdom come. I am so tired of being afraid.

The next thing I hear is Frank's voice. "You've got to see this," he announces. He's sitting up, looking out the door of the tent.

His hair sticks up alarmingly, and his face is orange. I pull myself forward on my elbows, and what I see through the door is a lake of fire.

In the sunrise, flares of gold and orange and lavender throw rays of light against the stony sky. Steam rises off the water in billows edged with gold. Across the marsh, I can make out a shadowy line of pines and the black silhouette of a bull moose. The air should smell of campfires and the ancient, story-laden dampness at the back of caves, but instead it is cool and fresh and smells of pine.

NOTES *f*rom THE PIG-BARN PATH

Campus Way runs under the brick arch of the Ag Sciences Building in Corvallis, past the greenhouses and the small-fruits building, crosses Thirty-fifth Street, and at that point becomes a macadam bike path that cuts through the fields all the way to Fifty-third. If they have special permits, Agriculture Department staff can drive down the path to the dairy barns and pig barns and over toward the horse pastures by the fairgrounds; otherwise, the path is reserved for people on bicycles or on foot.

Frank and I walk the pig-barn path as often as we can, whenever we can, which may turn out to be the end of the day, or the middle of the night, or first thing in the morning. Sometimes I write down what I have seen on one of these walks and put the dispatch into my desk drawer. I have appointed myself the reporter from the pig-barn path.

[135]

❧

This close to winter solstice, the sky is already dark by five in the afternoon. I can see rain slanting black across the last strip of light on the horizon. The wind, moving powerfully through the tops of oaks, fills the air with the sound of a great river. After days of rain, the fields are flooded on both sides of the path. I can hear cattle clanking against the gates in their stalls. The air smells like wood smoke and wet grass.

❧

There is a terrific storm in the valley tonight. Rain runs down my raincoat and soaks my jeans. I imagine fixing a gutter onto the hem of my coat to channel rain away from my pants into a drainpipe and onto the ground. Under the streetlights, rain hits the pavement at a thirty-degree angle and bounces into the air with a rush of sound and an explosion of spray, like surf in an ocean gale. "Great storm," people congratulate each other as they pass. "Great storm."

❧

A big flock of blackbirds and a single crow have landed on the path up ahead. They cover the roadbed and line up evenly along the fences and telephone wires. When we get too close, the flock lifts and moves twenty feet down the road, as if it were one thing, as if it were a frog. We walk that twenty feet and the flock hops again with a wash of air. How many times will it hop? Another twenty feet and it hops again. Finally, at some secret signal, the flock lifts off and divides in two, and each squadron peels away from the road, circles around us, and settles on the road behind.

❧

When we look straight up, we can see the sky. But down here, we walk in ground fog so thick that the road looks like a diving board, narrowing in the distance and dropping off into a gray sea. People pop out of the fog almost within touching distance. I can hear the wet sound of bike tires long before I see the bikes. Somewhere in the fog, a cow sneezes—a big, fluttering, wet sneeze.

Five A.M. I like to be out in early morning darkness. It excites me, as if I were going on a long journey, and frightens me, as if someone were going to the hospital. A car drives slowly along Thirty-fifth Street, slicking up the water on the road. I am curious about why the driver is out and whether he is coming home or going away. Does he feel cozy to be in his car or frightened to be out of bed?

The field to the south is impossibly green. Green, like katydids or Martians or the life force itself, as if the field were plugged into an electrical outlet—a green that would spark if you touched it, would set your sleeves on fire. Where the land rises and can't be plowed, alder thickets grow up, tangled and gray. Their branches bloom with tufts of lichen. From a distance the alders look like apple trees in bloom.

Where ryegrass pushes up against alders at the far edge of the field, blackberry brambles are engulfing an old pickup truck. Somebody has wired a plywood sign upright in the pickup bed. With binoculars, I can read the words: "The Wages of Sin," the sign says, "Is Death." Should that be the wages of sin *are* death, I wonder. But the wages of virtue is probably death too, and the brambles are already editing freely.

At the edge of the field, cows are walking single file toward the barn. Their udders bump gently against their ankles, their legs swish through deep grass. How much greener can the fields grow without exploding? These cows are black and white, and two of them have portholes in their sides. Agriculture students can pop off the portholes and look into the churning mass of chlorophyll and bacteria. I've always wanted to stick my head into this wilderness and breathe the distilled essence of spring inside a cow's stomach. When I suggested this to one of the Ag students in my class, she was disgusted. "It stinks in there," she said. I was sorry to learn this.

Undergraduates are out today on a field trip. They bunch near the fence, holding clipboards against their chests, poking at plants with the eraser ends of their pencils. A crow is cutting figure eights over their heads, but they don't see it. They are watching the professor press his thumbnail into the seed-head of a stalk of wheat.

Sometime yesterday or during the night, the sheep have been marked with spray paint. They all have parallel lines on their backs—blue, black, pink—and a few carry the proud cross of the Knights Templar. I think of sacrificial lambs, of crosses marked on doors, of pharaoh's men moving by torchlight, of revolution and betrayal, but these marks are only records marking experimental procedures completed—an examination, an injection.

The chest of one ram is painted red. The color runs down its neck, onto its abdomen, along the inside of its front legs. Frank says this is to mark the matings. When a ram mounts a ewe, the red dye comes off on her back—a scarlet letter that traces the tom-catting of the ram through the night. In the morning, the sun rises on a red stain spreading across the foggy pasture.

❧

Tonight is the county fair. On the pig-barn path in the dark, Frank and I can hear the music of the Smokin' Armadillos even though the fairgrounds are two miles away—just the bass chords in a four/four rhythm, pounding so profoundly that the music might be blood in my veins. When we look to the west, we can see a crescent moon and the lights of the Tilt-a-Whirl. Points of pink and green and yellow rise and fall, and with each fall comes a distant chord of human screams.

❧

Camas is in bloom in the ditches, a drift of dark blue flowers hidden deep in the grasses. I have read that camas once covered these hillsides like cloud shadows in the spring, and Calapooya families came from distant valleys to dig the roots for food. Now camas survives only in ditches and boggy places where tractors can't go.

This is a domesticated land: cleared, plowed, leveled, pH-tested, neutralized, fertilized, planted to a single crop selectively bred to grow to a uniform height and form seed-heads at a uniform time. Wildness presses against the back fence, reaches out from the oaks and alder trees, but cattle—also bred to grow to a uniform height and weight—stick their heads over the fences and shear off the branches.

For years, the battle between wild and tame has waged under these fences, where ryegrass invades the little patches of deer fern and horsetails, and thick moss chokes back the grass. Graduate students sally forth to spray a stripe of herbicide under the fence row, creating a bare hollow along the fence—a narrow no-man's-land that fills with water in the winter and keeps the ferns at bay.

❧

A few summers ago, our daughter worked for the Crop Science Department. Her job was to walk the experimental wheat fields, uprooting any stalk of wheat that was taller than the others. Day after day, for miles and miles, she pulled nonconforming stalks up by the roots before they could set seed. When she was done, her fields were as level and smooth as AstroTurf.

The domestication of the animals. The domestication of the land. How will we resist the domestication of the spirit?

❧

Today the Brewer's blackbirds are lined up on the electric wires like pearls on a necklace, evenly spaced. If an extra bird floats down and shoulders its way onto the wire, birds in both directions sidle away until the spacing is even again. Nature has its own order. The flock makes a constant chatcheting noise that fills the air like sawdust.

❧

The sheep have stripes on their faces, big swaths of fuchsia paint smeared along the ridgeline between their eyes. I stop to figure it out. A single sheep turns slowly toward me, a blade of grass hanging off its lower lip like Humphrey Bogart's cigarette. It looks blankly in my direction. I study the eyes, trying to see a spark inside. Set deep inside fleece, the eyes do not reflect light. "Are you in there?" I ask. No answer. Dull eyes fade back into fleece and suddenly the animal's yellow ear-tags are staring at me—widespread, round, glowing yellow eyes—a transformation that startles me. I step back from the fence. All the sheep's heads swing toward me and a whole flock of beings with widespread yellow eyes is watching me with a steady gaze—aliens in sheep's clothing, grazing in the field by the lambing barns, a robotic, extraterrestrial awareness in their plastic eyes.

≈

Now there's rioting on the pig-barn path. Crewcut fields of ryegrass stand in ordered ranks, their lines straight. But already the wild roses have broken down the fence, and hawthorn thickets press in behind them. Blackberry brambles are sending out long prickly stems that grow at horror-show rates. They reach out and wind around bushes, pulling themselves along the ground like animals with broken backs. Bindweed burrows into the field, poking up sprouts to reconnoiter. Scotch-broom thickets flash with flowers that snap if you touch them and slap pollen all over your finger. Mock-orange engulfs the path with sweetness. Great masses of cow parsnips, hairy and smelly, press against the edges of the field and spill onto the grass, scattering pollen.

The professors are doing their best to keep order, with their genetically engineered ryegrass and multiple-choice exams. But this is going to be a long struggle with no clear winner, and I'm rooting for the weeds.

THE MAN WITH A STUM*p*
WHERE HIS HEAD SHOULD BE

When you're a middle-aged professor, a mother twice over, and fully five-and-a-half feet tall, it's hard to disguise yourself as a little kid. But I didn't want some lady to say "Aren't you a little old for trick-or-treat?" so I gave my costume a lot of thought. The real stumper was my height. All fall, I had mulled over ways to make myself shorter, but everything I thought of would have forced me into contortions that would have killed me after a couple of blocks. Then, one day early in October, right in the middle of a faculty meeting, the solution struck me: When you're a tall person trying to look short, the trick is to disguise yourself as a short person trying to look tall. I could be a huge Cyclops. But no: When kids think of monsters, classical Greek monsters don't come immediately to mind. Maybe Godzilla would do the trick. Finally I decided to be a giant murder victim, beheaded.

The idea was so disgusting, it couldn't lose. I made a neck stump out of foam and cut cardboard into broad shoulders to wear on the top of my head. Then I draped a shirt and tweed coat over the shoulders, tied a necktie around the stump, and cut little eye-holes in the shirt. I stood back with squinty eyes and assessed my creation. Needs blood, I decided. So I splashed red paint on the stump and dripped it drooling down the front of the shirt—what I thought was a nice nine-year-old touch.

My second problem was getting into character. Somehow I had to acquire the vague *where am I?* step of a child who can't see past her mask. It took discipline to suppress all my middle-aged efficiency—*let's just get the candy and get on with it.* I practiced milling around and gazing at the sky like a person who is seldom out after dark. I tried saying "thank you" in a terrible, beheaded voice, because children always say *thank you* when they trick-or-treat. In front of the mirror, I practiced saying "trick or treat, smell my feet" and collapsing with laughter, holding onto my stump.

I didn't want to go alone, but my children were appalled, and Frank was having nothing to do with this. He said he would offer consultation on anatomy, and that was it. So after several days of bargaining and offers of increasingly large shares of the candy, I finally talked my sister into coming along. My sister is a forty-two-year-old schoolteacher, even taller than I am, but with the right costume, she would probably pass. She decided to be a giant chicken. The murder victim and the chicken. We wore sneakers, so we could run if we needed to, and gloves to hide our wedding rings and middle-aged hands. At the last minute, we added an accomplice, a young man who will have to remain unnamed. His job was to stand in the shadows on the sidewalk and nag. "Did you say thank you to the nice lady? Watch the jack-o'-lanterns so you don't set yourself on fire!"

We got peanut butter cups from the man next door, and Tootsie Pops from the Martins. The Davenports were giving out raisins, which is an awful thing to do to a kid. Skittles, a pumpkin-faced sucker, a cinnamon bear in a plastic wrapper, red licorice. At the end of that block we stopped to check our loot and laugh into our bags.

We knew that the most dangerous moment would come at the big house on the corner, Mrs. Schaefer's. Mrs. Schaefer is ninety years old and sharp as a knife, and she doesn't miss a trick. If I don't wear a coat in the rain, if I prune my dogwood too severely, if I'm coming home late, she raps her knuckles against her kitchen window and wrinkles her face into a warning. We stopped under a streetlight to check our costumes and then marched up to her door. Swinging the door open before I could finish grunting "trick or treat," Mrs. Schaefer drew back and cried out, "Oh my goodness, who could this awful, ugly monster be? And who is his friend, the . . ." She paused. "Duck," she said doubtfully. "Chicken," my sister and I said in unison. Mrs. Schaefer stared shrewd and eagle-eyed past the porch light. "Come into the light where I can see you. Do you live on this street?" I couldn't say a word, so I just clutched my throat and made a strangling, gurgling sound. She leaned closer, trying to gauge the size of the chicken. This was more than we could take. We stumbled off the porch and ran into the darkness between houses, finding the way as well as we could with eyeholes that kept jostling out of position. We stood behind the arborvitae for a long minute, breathing hard. Then, terrified and triumphant, we cut across the block to trick-or-treat at the fraternity houses, where we could take candy from my students.

All in all, we each got away with an orange plastic sack of loot, maybe five pounds of candy. When we got back to the house, we dumped the bags out on the dining room table. Gloating over the heaps of contraband, bragging about our derring-do, sorting the candy into piles, trading raisins for suckers, fending off our children and husbands, we drank beer in triumph.

It's a heady feeling, to fool people so thoroughly, to risk exposure, to pull it off, to try to buffalo Mrs. Schaefer, who scrutinizes my costume changes and is suspicious of each one: Tuesday nights, I'm a PTA president. Saturdays, I'm a soccer team mother. Sundays, I'm the gardener. Weekdays, I'm a philosophy professor. I wear dark suits and white blouses (because I read in a magazine that people respect you more if you look like a nun), tailored jackets with Frankenstein shoulders, high-heeled shoes, silky stockings. Day after day, I stand in costume in front of my students and speak the big words and the complicated sentences. Usually I'm proud of the way I can metamorphose from mother to wife to professor, just by changing my clothes. But sometimes in class I'm terrified I'll forget my lines and the students will say, "Look, it's the PTA president!" And what if they discover that the PTA president is only nine years old? Or that the nine-year-old has no head?

Last week, I was introduced to the new dean of education. Shaking my hand a second too long, he narrowed his eyes and said, "A philosopher? You sure don't look like a philosopher." I pulled my hand away. He stared at me, trying to see into the darkness behind my eyeholes. I quickly checked my costume, unnerved and angry. Dark suit, white blouse. The more he scrutinized me, the madder I got. It would have served him right if I had gone home, put on that big tweed jacket, and reappeared as the man with a stump where his head should be. I would have charged at him with my arms outspread, making horrid gasping noises, and he would have howled in fear and run right out of the humanities building into the street.

Do other people go through life adjusting their eyeholes? Do other people keep to the dark corners of the room, one minute terrified of exposure and the next minute astounded at the success of the fraud? Do men wake up at night and wonder if they are still children? It's a strain, wearing all these costumes, playing all these parts. I keep thinking that some day I will play a role so perfectly that I will be transformed into that character, but it hasn't happened yet. In the meantime, I come home from the university, take off my jacket, spread the homework assignments on the dining room table, and rejoice that I made it through another round of lectures without setting my costume on fire.

THE ONLY *p*LACE LIKE THIS

As a bald eagle coasts over his head, a little boy walks along the boardwalk toward school, wearing a life jacket, clutching a handful of daffodils. He passes an old man on a four-wheeler.

"Hiya," the boy says. "How are you today?"

"Home, sick in bed," the old man announces. Then without waiting for the boy to figure out the joke, he laughs, downshifts, and trundles off, rattling the planks of the boardwalk past the Cold Storage Plant and a boarded-up house. By the post office, a little dog is sitting square in the middle of the walkway, not moving. The old man stops, turns off his engine, and devotes ten minutes to the project of scratching the dog. Close by, two men in yellow rain-pants lean over the railing, talking in low voices, watching a school of herring. Frank and I sit on a wooden bench in front of the restaurant, looking across the boardwalk to the inlet and the mountains beyond. Our backs are erasing "borscht" from the chalkboard menu.

Wildland shoulders in on the little town from all directions, jagged snow-covered peaks and fjords as deep as the mountains are high. Because the mountains plunge so steeply into the sea, the town is built on stilts over the water. Buildings line up on both sides of a boardwalk that runs along the bluffs, graying wooden cottages connected by narrow planks with railings. Even the school sits at the end of a pier, on posts above the tidal flats. Twice each day, tides move in under the town, and twice each day they move out again, stranding starfish.

The nearest road is seventy miles away. When the weather is good—which it rarely is—a floatplane might land at the dock and off-load a fisherman, or a dog, or some groceries. We flew in on yesterday's floatplane, imported from outside to teach in the school for a few days. Low clouds forced us to fly below the cliffs along arms of the sea, skimming close to the waves like a pelican. The ferry comes only once a month. When the schoolteacher's piano arrived by barge, the town turned out to haul the piano up the gangway and along the boardwalk on the back of the only suitable vehicle in town, the garbage ATV. Now the teacher trades piano lessons for halibut and jam and considers herself ahead in the bargain.

This little town is home to 160 people, more or less, people who take the word "home" seriously. When I ask my writing students what marks this place as home, the seven children in the high school put their heads together and make me a list:

> The Boardwalk
> Boringness
> Dogs barking
> My boat

TOO MUCH RAIN.
Bears
The restaurant
The river.

I press them for the names of the inlet, the restaurant, the river, the bears, and they debate for some time, but really, the question makes no sense. What's the use of proper names, when there's only one of each? But the children consult among themselves and tell me that the bears are brown bears. They wander into town in April looking for something to eat, but head back to the mountains when the snows melt. "They have their space and we have ours and it works out pretty good," says a student. All the same, she spent the night with a friend, having been warned not to walk home past the place a bear had been seen. When townspeople visit each other at night, they carry cowbells and pepper spray. And when word comes round that a bear is on the boardwalk just past the church, the teacher leaves her meeting and walks home to bring her dog inside.

There are more docks than boardwalks in this town, and more boats than houses. Amidst the working boats, a couple of sailboats hunker down under blue tarps. "Tourists," the sheriff explains. He laughs, holding his cigarette between his forefinger and thumb. Lacking much business in the crime department, he has joined us on the bench. We look out together at the boats in the moorage and give the sun time to work its way into our shoulders. "Had one woman stand here on her boat and ask how many feet above sea level we were. Had another lady fly in over the glacier and ask what we did with all that styrofoam. 'We mine it,' I told her, 'and ship it south for picnic coolers.'" He laughs again and then it's quiet on the dock except for the sound of waterfalls streaming down the mountains across the inlet.

"I don't know why they call it tourist season, if we're not allowed to shoot 'em." But he's only joking, just running through his repertoire of dumb-tourist jokes, and here comes the next one: "Some guy asked me how much rain was forecast, and I said I expected it to fill the inlet about eight more feet by suppertime." Then the law looks over at us, so obviously strangers, and remembers his manners. "Aw, a few tourists aren't so bad. As long as they go home."

A boy runs past, carrying a fishing pole. A few others bunch on the boardwalk, jostling and wrestling without ever dismounting from their bikes. Their parents are out on the boardwalk too, gathered in small groups to talk and tease, enjoying the first clear evening in a long, long time. "I don't think I'd like to live anywhere else but here," a sixteen-year-old tells me. "Doesn't seem all that nice in other places. Except maybe I'll go to college, if there's a college in a place like this."

What she doesn't know is that she may live in the only place like this.

This was a company town, built for packing salmon in 1930. For decades the people got by, prosperity ebbing and flowing with the schools of herring that brought in the chinook. But last year, the long-line fisherman who doubles as town manager received a letter over his fax machine: *The fish plant will close on Friday.* Word spread quickly the length of the boardwalk, past the wet-goods store, past the storefront "steambaths and showers," past the bar-and-grill and the restaurant, past the fire station and the boatyard where crab traps pile up off-season, to the row of little company houses along the boardwalk, the school, the river, and the end of town.

Some families moved away. Some fathers left to get jobs outside, leaving their families behind. Other parents divided their children among the neighbors and went off to find work. Somebody cobbled together financing to run the fish plant for a few months a year, other people set up their boats for halibut, off-loading their catch on fish-buying boats. The people who remain in this little town get by whatever way they can and wonder what will happen next. On the docks, we overhear the worried conversations, the patched-together plans. In the school, I listen to the children. They want to know about the Seattle Sonics, but I can't help them. Their parents are holding on to a way of life as tightly as the town clings to the mountainside, but they know it's going to take more than a life jacket to keep their children from drifting away.

So it's complicated when a corporation from outside announces plans to build a floating lodge near the town and fly in paying guests. The site the corporation has chosen is close enough to town that the people will see floatplanes coming and going, day after day, bringing in people, taking out trophy fish. The corporation plans to moor its lodge in a place rare and wonderful, anchoring its cables to pilings in front of the only beach in the fjord, a beach where townspeople have always come to dig for clams, and where long-line fishermen—grandfathers and fathers and sons—angle for salmon and halibut. The place where mothers bring their children for picnics, running out to the beach in skiffs.

"The people don't want the lodge," says a songwriter whose family has lived in the town from the beginning, when the first corporation came in three generations ago. "None of us want it. It won't bring *us* any jobs. And even if it did, they wouldn't be worth it. But what can we do?" And sure enough, when a representative of the corporation comes to town, the people are polite, the way they are polite to the bears and the occasional tourist. People don't argue here, said a fourteen-year-old girl. "In a town as small as this, you can't just say whatever you're thinking."

But the people know the value of what they would be giving up. Scarcity raises the value of anything. As peace and solitude and wildlands disappear under bulldozers in the south, their price increases proportionately. Peace becomes a commodity, like board feet of cedar or kilos of frozen fish. Solitude is precious. Unspoiled beauty sells for a premium. Anyone who figures out how to extract these resources will make a fortune.

The townspeople call a meeting, gathering in the town hall just down from the dry goods store. "What the corporation plans to do," a bearded man says, "is take the peace and solitude that belong to this community, the same peace and solitude the people have been saving for their children." They will take it without asking, without giving anything in return, as if it belonged to them. Then they will package it and sell it to strangers for something around $2,500, a five-day package deal. "There's a word for this," a woman says, holding her son on her hip. "But I can't put my finger on it. Isn't it 'theft'?"

The schoolteacher pushes back her chair and stands up. "This isn't about just one fishing lodge," she says. "It's about this one and the next one and the next. Is this the kind of life we want? Is this what we want for the children?"

"I wouldn't know," says the corporate representative. "That's a philosophical question."

But the people know. What they want for their children are salmon and yellow cedar, the River, the Inlet, and a little town where wooden houses stand on stilts above great schools of fish. A place you know is home because, as a teenager explained it to me, when you open the door "there's a row of boots and raincoats and some firewood, and your little brother is waiting to beat you up." A place where bears roll boulders on the beach, sucking up crabs and sculpin. Where gardens grow in milk crates stacked above the tide—daffodils and garlic, and rhubarb for pies. A place where women's voices call to children across the docks, and salt wind carries the laughter of men. A place where people can make a living, but not a fortune. A place where enough is great riches.

CANOEING ON THE LINE *of* A SONG

t's an unsettling thing, to come so suddenly into a new landscape. Jackfish, Beartrap. Snowbank, Basswood. Moose River. The kitchen table is a chaos of yellow-tabbed guidebooks, forest service pamphlets, canoe route maps. I scan the names of lakes, matching them with their descriptions, trying to figure out where to go. On the Superior-Quetico canoe map, the blue lakes look like storm clouds bucking northeasterly winds. I can read the shapes of the lakes from the contour lines on the McKenzie maps, but there are no symbols marking the smell of the hillsides or the slant of light in the forest. For all I can tell, the water could reflect thick stands of balsam fir, sweet and dark, or open hillsides layered with hardwoods in blazing color, or bare rock ledges ringing under heavy waves.

I try not to let the unfamiliarity bother me. After all, we've gone to a great deal of trouble to get to a new place, driving all the way from Oregon to Minnesota to spend the fall near the Boundary Waters. I'm sure that after I get my bearings I'll come to know and love these lakes, as I came to love my Oregon rivers. But I'm uneasy now, and I wish I knew one landmark or lake. Everything else could be measured by that.

Layers of maps. Portages measured in rods—a sixteen-and-a-half-foot distance I understand in my mind, but can't feel in my feet. Pickerel Lake and Rock Island Lake and Prairie Portage. I'm grateful for these place-names; at least they give me a hint of what the land is like. Entry points. Permits. I flip pages. *Paddle to the west end of Knife Lake where the river flows one and one-quarter miles west to Carp Lake. Big Knife Portage bypasses a nasty stretch of rapids on the Knife River.* Does the description refer to the sort of nasty I'm used to in Oregon, or is there a special kind of Minnesota nasty? How will I learn about the degrees of not-quite-nasty that I will have to navigate in my narrow canoe? How will I predict the direction of the wind?

I pull out the map on the bottom of the pile and lay it over the rest. Map H, Saganaga and Seagull Lakes Area. More blue lakes, more dotted lines. I pull out another map, Mountain–Pine Lakes. A string of lakes abruptly stops my eye, and I lean over to look more closely. Here is a canoe route from Lake Duncan to Clearwater to the Bearskin, up along the Border Trail. I trace the route with my finger. Can it be? I know this place as well as I know the house I grew up in. This canoe route is a line from a song my mother used to sing.

I try to remember the words to the song. *It's the flash of paddle blades agleaming in the sun. A canoe softly slipping by the shore.* I fumble with the next line, but I don't think my mother would mind; she was a great one for *la-la*-ing through a song. *It's the smell of pine and bracken coming on the wind.* I'm missing a couple of lines here. But now, the chorus, the canoe route, laid out lake to lake: *By Lake Duncan to Clearwater to the Bearskin I will go, where you see the loon and hear its plaintive wail.*

This canoe route is the background music of my childhood. My mother sang the song softly, a lullaby, as she sat at the foot of the bed and my sisters and I drifted off to sleep. She hummed it as she dusted shelves and thought of other things. She sang it as she drove downtown, her elbow sticking out the car window, her purse on the seat beside her. When we were sick, or lonely, or homesick, this is the song she would sing to comfort us. And now this music has become a dotted line on my map, a place I can find.

For her, I think it was all a dream, a song about a fantasy world of clear lakes and sweet pines. Standing at the stove in Cleveland, stirring the tuna fish into the noodles, singing songs she learned when she was a Girl Scout, my mother had no way of knowing that this was a real place etched by glaciers in granite. She never knew—I'm sure she didn't—that this was a place with real loons, genuine plaintive wails.

I will go there. I will go there tomorrow. I will canoe along the line of the song. Then sitting on the edge of Bearskin Lake, I'll sing all the verses I can bring to mind. Quietly, in a voice as uncertain as memory, I will sing to the tuna fish casserole, to the loons, to the white pines, to a woman whose songs had to be enough.

I circle the Bearskin on my map. I have a fixed point, and I can go from here.

INCOMING TIDE

Seven A.M. on Easter morning, and time for the sunrise service. The congregation—just me so far—sits quietly on a damp pew, soaking up moisture from barnacles and bladder wrack. A few more parishioners float in, a gull, a bufflehead duck. They flutter their feathers, shoulder to rump, and we settle in, waiting for trumpets. But as we listen, I realize that the bright tones of the varied thrush have been sounding since dawn. Choir members are clearing their throats and sailing in, the wind humming in their wing feathers. Feet-first, they crash-land on the bay, then smooth their vestments as they float toward shore. They gabble and clack, tuning up, but any moment I expect them to order their ranks and begin the opening hymn. The bay rises and falls in low swells, flexing stained-glass pictures of islands and cloud-blowing peaks and Frank in the distance, fly fishing in water up to his knees. At unexpected times and places, all across the tidal flat, clams shoot streams of water high into the air, high enough to catch light just now coming through cracks between the mountains.

There are six hard-boiled eggs in my pack, some frozen sausages, a bag of jelly beans, and a cellophane packet of marshmallow chickens. In the town, mothers will be combing their daughters' hair and folding down the lace-trimmed edges of their socks. A preacher will be sticking yellow Post-it notes at appropriate places in the New Testament, and grandmothers will be poking cloves through the skins of Easter hams. A pair of goldeneyes glides by, rubbing shoulders. Barnacles click all around me in their pews as if they were cracking gum.

My family's Easter tradition was to hide baskets filled with candy, a hard-boiled egg, and a new pair of socks. But we were a competitive family, and my father especially saw everything in life as an intellectual challenge. So, the older we got, the harder it was to find the baskets. One year my basket was suspended by a string inside the chimney. Another year, my father poured the contents of my basket into a cooking pot in the pantry and put on the lid. He unzipped a sofa pillow, took out the stuffing, replaced it with an Easter basket, and sat down on it. He unscrewed a ceiling light, set the basket inside the globe, and screwed the lamp back to the ceiling. We had Easter baskets in the garbage can, and Easter baskets in the raisin bran box. Even now I think of Easter as an intellectual contest with my father—he's trying to keep it hidden and I'm trying to find it, taking the house apart, finally wondering just what this basket of candy is really worth. And to be honest, this is the way I have come to think of religion.

Somebody is going to have to give me a clue—tell me if I'm hot or cold—or I'll go without. There is a limit.

We always went to church on Easter when I was a child, walking out of the hot sun into a church foyer as cool as a cave, past a painting of Jesus who, with his wavy hair parted in the middle, his big rabbit's eyes, looked a lot like my sister. We trooped down the aisle while the organ played and my mother paused now and then to touch the shoulders of her friends. The air coming through open windows smelled of rejoicing, of new-cut grass, of babies, and when the organ sent forth Beethoven's bass chords, the milky air trembled, and we could feel it in our feet, through the soles of our patent leather shoes. We turned the pages of the hymnal awkwardly in cotton gloves, finally finding the right page only after the singing had begun, but it didn't matter because we knew the words by heart.

The minister told us that after Adam and Eve had eaten the apple, they heard the sound of God walking in the garden in the cool of the day. I would eat a hundred apples, a million apples, I remember saying as we walked home past the sandstone bank building and the Civil War monument in the park, if that meant I could hear the sound of God walking. My sisters and I debated for some time and finally decided that God would most likely make the sound of a giant, crushing hollyhocks and scattering birds and raising furious clouds of honeybees, but we couldn't be sure. And what would it smell like, the smell of God walking by? Shaving cream was all I could think of, but I knew that was a dumb answer because everybody said God had a beard. So the sound and smell of God remained a mystery, and it has been decades since I have stepped inside a church.

But now I have met a man who claims to have seen God.

"Well, tell me about it," I said.

"It was in an airplane on a flight to Chicago," he said. "A routine flight, nothing to tell me anything was out of the ordinary. Suddenly, as I looked down the aisle, everything was beautiful. The man sitting next to me was beautiful. Understand: He was quite ugly. In fact as I sat down, I had said to myself, 'this man is really ugly,' but as I looked at him, he was beautiful. It had to do with light, I think, the way the backs of the seats struck me as beautiful, and the television monitors, hanging from the ceiling. It's hard to describe, but I can tell you that tears were rolling down my cheeks as I understood how ordinary things, those little paper towels they stick to the tops of the seats with Velcro, were beautiful, the handle on the window blind. This went on for a long time, maybe forty-five minutes. I just sat there crying, seeing the inside of that airplane, understanding for the first time that everything was holy, and that I had been blessed to see it with my own eyes."

"Really!" I said, and as I thought about it, I felt a little stupid. Because something like this happens to me all the time. Not on airplanes. But other places. In forests, or huckleberry patches. I'll be hiking along under the hemlocks and suddenly the light will stream in sideways and every leaf lights up and I'm stopped in midstride, overwhelmed by how beautiful the forest has become. Women in sweatsuits walk briskly by, swinging their arms from their shoulders like storm troopers. They look at me funny, and fathers take hold of their children's hands, but what am I supposed to do? Sometimes the natural world gives you a gift so beautiful, so precious, that all you can do is stand there and cry. But I never actually thought of this as religion. All the same, the thought is an interesting one, and now I'm trying to look around me a little differently, keep an open mind.

Gradually the tide slides in and green slime on the rocks begins to rise and take shape. Leaves of sea lettuce separate and float, touched by filtered sun. The stalked anemones open like cauliflowers, although I have never seen cauliflowers so full of light. A starfish that had been a purple splotch on the gravel lifts itself on a thousand tiny tiptoes and dances slowly away, waving its arms expressively like a toddler learning ballet. I make a quick assessment of the height of my boots, jump off my rock just before the tides would have stranded me entirely, and walk up the flat, over the eelgrass beds, into the salt marsh, where each blade of grass bends seaward, pointing to the incoming tide.

Frank wades to shore, breaking down his rod. In a ring of stones, we build a fire and cook the sausages. It took me a long time to pick out just the right maple-flavored sausages at the grocery store last night, but these were as close as I could get to my father's traditional Easter ham. We eat the sausage and the hardboiled eggs and some of the marshmallow chickens.

After we've finished eating, we sit silently, watching, while the tide moves in, filing slowly up the little channels until the whole bay spreads and lifts every frond of seaweed, each blade of marsh grass, every hemlock needle and stranded log. To tell the truth, I feel a little lifted too.

DEAD RECKONING

Dead reckoning is navigation by deductive logic. When you can't see the stars, when you don't have any landmarks, you can sometimes figure out where you are by knowing where you started, how long you have traveled, and what course you have taken. Columbus used dead reckoning to find the Caribbean four times, measuring his speed with rhyming chants, an hourglass, and the beating of his pulse—but that doesn't mean it's easy. With dead reckoning, everything depends on knowing where you were in the first place—the *last well-determined position,* the Coast Guard says. Then you need to know what direction you are going in, which is not always clear at sea where wind and currents pull a boat off-course. You need to know how fast you are moving, and this is tricky too; there is *speed*—how fast you are going relative to the water, and then there is *speed made good*—speed relative to the earth. When everything is moving under you, the difference between what you intend and what you actually accomplish can be the width of a shoal.

"So can you point through the window and tell me where to start?" I had asked the clerk in the marine supply store in Prince Rupert harbor. He gave me a long look, but he closed the cash register drawer, walked to the window, and pointed. "Right there, between those two islands. See the channel?" In fact, there were a dozen islands and as many channels. "No," I said. Reading his face, I could see questions that reflected the doubt in my own mind. *Deductive* reckoning, *ded.* reckoning, *dead* reckoning.

I lean against my truck, trying to remember everything I once knew about finding my way. My daughter is bending over brand-new marine charts spread on the hood. She is penciling in vectors, drawing a careful zigzag line through passages between scattered islands. The harbor smells of gasoline and fish-packing plants— salty seaweed drying on the rocks, gutted fish, bubbly lines of gills and pale sausagy intestines drifting on the tide. These are smells I know and love. I do not want to leave this harbor. Erin looks up from the charts. "We can do this," she says.

I sit down on the dock. This is so complicated. We were supposed to have launched on inland water and motored up passages between islands entirely protected from the sea. Among inland passages, weather would be no threat, and finding our way along fjords would be as easy as walking a ditch. But the back road to the launch site is closed for bridge repairs, and here we are in a deep-sea port instead—the northernmost harbor on the British Columbia coast—plotting an alternative course that will take us miles into the Pacific before we eventually arrive at the inland passages. We can buoy-hop for some of the time, but we're going to have to do most of this by dead reckoning because we don't know these waters and we have no way to tell one island from another. There will be reefs in the lee of the islands, but worse yet, on the long reach when we round the headland at the entrance, it's wide open ocean. I'm not convinced this is wise.

"We'll take our time loading up—launching the boat, stowing gear, getting gas," Erin says. "We'll take a run around the harbor. We'll stop and reconsider before each step, and both of us have veto power. Either one of us says *no,* that's it." I bristle at being the one who needs to be reassured—that's a mother's job, not her daughter's—and really, my preference would be to sit down and cry for a little while here and think this over. But I'll go along with her plan: If we're going to make this run, I want to make it in daylight, and if we're not, I want time to find a camp.

Erin backs the trailer down the ramp. Honestly, this might be the dumbest thing I've ever done. Loosening the winch, I unhook the boat and take hold of the bowline. Erin backs in until the trailer is completely submerged and bubbles rise from the taillights; then she hits the brakes. Slowly the boat floats backward off the trailer. I know better than to take a twenty-foot fiberglass skiff into the open sea. I tie the boat to the dock. Erin accelerates up the ramp and parks the rig in the parking lot. She walks back down the ramp, carrying four food buckets at once. If conditions are perfect, this'll be easy, but with wind or fog? I carry down the chart case and an extra anchor. Erin jumps in the boat and starts to stow gear in the cabin. This is the north Pacific, not some little pond. I hand in two kayaks and Erin straps each one to the rail. My daughter is twenty-four years old. She helped drive this boat in the inland passages last summer. She is experienced and skilled. I hand her the kayak paddles. But she's the same person who sideswiped the ticket booth at the drive-in movie when she was sixteen, and never even knew it. Looking around to be sure we haven't forgotten anything, I lock the truck and carry down the dry bags. I cast off the lines and lower myself into the boat. I guess the worst that could happen is we would drown. Erin looks at me, sits a minute on my silence, waits another minute. Then she whoops and turns the key.

The engine never starts on the first crank. Two hundred horsepower sits there looking stupid. A couple of fishermen lean out the window of their seiner and whistle. But on the second crank, the engine churns and spits and Erin is backing away from the dock and we are actually going to do this.

It's four o'clock in the afternoon. The sky is overcast. It's sixty degrees Fahrenheit. The wind is ten knots from the northwest. There is a line of fog at the western horizon. With the Prince Rupert channel marker bearing 145 degrees, distant 200 yards, we take departure. The bay is black, littered with piles of seaweed and fish offal, amputated logs, scuffed and yellow, and buoys marking crab pots. "Flotsam and jetsam," I shout over the thrum of the engine, but Erin laughs. "You've got it wrong," she shouts. "Jetsam is what you throw overboard to keep from sinking. Flotsam is what floats on the water after you've sunk." I stand in the stern in a cloud of gasoline fumes, absorbing the vocabulary lesson.

Gradually, the harbor goes hazy and the mountains fade from green to gray. When I look ahead, all I see is a confusion of islands and leads that might be passages or might be bays. Behind us, our wake parts the sea neatly into two curling walls, and between the walls, the prop churns the water into a wide white path clearly drawn on the sea. I remember teaching our children to read maps this way—not asking them to plot a trip on the map, but showing them how to mark where we had been. Two little kids strapped in the backseat of the car, leaning over a triple-A map, holding yellow markers in their fists.

Erin has the charts spread out, all ordered near to far. Between shoals in the passage, she picks a way carefully from buoy to buoy, turning to meet the wakes of incoming trawlers. Then we're crossing a bay, motoring slowly to the southwest, squinting into light that gleams on the swell, hiding deadheads and drift nets. We pass a small Tlingit village, then steer around the bedded reefs of an island and move into another channel. A seiner churns by, trailing diesel fumes and a strand of seagulls.

I have put myself in charge of spotting buoys, the markers that connect the charts to the sea. This is the issue—right here. Deductive logic is fine, as far as it goes. But you can't figure everything out in advance, plotting your course on the chart and then chugging along the pencil line as if it were the real thing. Now and then, you have to get a fix, you have to learn where you are, not by where you expect to be, but by what your senses tell you, what you learn from the shape of the horizon. With binoculars, I pick up a pillar buoy dead ahead.

But now we motor from the protection of the island into the open sea. The bow rises on each swell and drops with a thud into each trough, lifting a screen of water that smacks on the windshield. Erin eases off the throttle, slowing the boat, raising my pulse, skidding up the back of each wave, then sliding the boat off the side and plowing through the slick. She must know I'm afraid, because she points to a peak vague on the horizon and then to a headland marked on the chart. "Do you see the mountain there?"

she asks. "When we're to the lee of that, we're in protected water. After that, it's a cruise."

When did this happen, that Erin knows how to do this better than I do? How did it happen that she has coaxed me into making this trip, when last I looked I was giving her M&M's to bribe her up a mountain trail? Why should she be unafraid, when my heart is scrabbling against my ribs like a rat in a box?

Erin's paying attention now, ducking her head to look through the swath of windshield where a wiper is swatting back and forth. Here in the entrance to the sound, the tide is running out and the swells are rolling in. Where the forces collide, they throw the wreckage of waves high into the air and the boat dives and pivots in the chop. Erin heads into the biggest waves, altering course to keep water from washing in on her stern, doing her best to keep slop from throwing the boat around and smacking over the bow. I think I see the blow of a whale, but it might be sea spray, and I don't look twice. I don't want to lose concentration on the task at hand, even though it's Erin who is handling the boat and my main responsibility now is to be afraid for both of us.

I've just about decided we are rooted to this pitching place, when suddenly the seas are calm and I'm surprised by the smell of hemlock and the warmth of the breeze. I can see individual trees on what had been a vaguely dark shore, and there are gulls on the rocks, pecking at their feet. I take off my raincoat and stow it in the cabin.

Erin looks around carefully, then turns again to the charts. Now that we're inland, the challenge is to find the way through a maze of channels and inlets to the particular island where we will meet the others tomorrow. Dusk is coming on, but it will be a long dusk in the northern summer. Slowly now, no hurry. If it gets dark we'll just find an anchorage and lay over for the night. I feel the calm of the water working on me, settling in my shoulders, and the weepy exhaustion and exultation that come with relief.

It's slack low tide, so the passage is a trough eighteen feet below the shoreline, and fallen trees jut over the water, trailing ropes of bullwhip kelp. We motor past islands perched high on basalt pedestals topped with hemlocks and huckleberries. Through a narrow passage we motor slowly, the engine noise echoing off granite cliffs, then around a hidden reef and into an inlet and on north. The darker it gets, the more closely I scan the shore for moorages, studying the charts to learn if the bottom is rock or sand. I climb onto the bow and coil the anchor line. We see eagles now, immense dark birds with heads and tails that disappear against the cloud cover: eagles sitting on snags, or on rocks, or soaring under overhanging trees.

As we round a narrow point, there, on high ground, is a black wolf. Erin cuts the engine and we coast to a stop, silence catching up to us and sliding over our heads. The wolf abruptly turns and disappears. We stare at the place it had been—the matted grass, the algae-slicked rock, a pocket of sand. Then I climb down from the bow while Erin comes out of the cockpit. We meet in a long hug, as if we were meeting in an airport, as if we had each come from very far away to get to this place.

Venus has risen over the mountains by the time we reach the island we're seeking. It's too dark to set up camp. At tomorrow's high tide, we'll off-load the gear onto the island and pitch the tent on the point. Frank and Jonathan will fly in, and we'll put out the crab traps and fish for salmon and kayak in and out of bays. But for tonight, we'll have to sleep onboard.

Erin brings the boat slowly into the narrow passage where we will set anchor. When the boat is in just the right place, I drop the bow anchor and signal Erin to put the boat in reverse. As she backs the boat away, I pay out line until I feel the anchor grab. A hard tug to be sure it's set, and I let the boat pull out the rest of the line. "That's it," I call, and Erin turns off the engine. She walks to the stern and lowers the second anchor. While I pull in rope at the bow, she pays out the stern line until the boat is midway between the two anchors. Erin tests the anchor's set, throws out more line, and wraps the rope around a cleat. I secure the forward anchor, leaving enough slack in the lines that the rising tide can't lift the boat and carry it away with its anchors hanging below like fishing lures; but not so much slack that currents can wash the boat onto rocks and damage the propeller.

Setting an anchor is something I know how to do. The slow motion dance, the forward and back of it, the partnership, the soft movement of the tides past a boat at rest, the sureness of our hold on the earth—there's a joy in this, a kind of homemaking, and when the anchors are set and the engine is finally quiet, silence settles around us like snow and a sea lion exhales somewhere in the passage. We tie our kayaks to long lines and push them overboard. Shoving aside the rest of the gear, we spread sleeping bags on the deck and slide in.

Evening. Bedtime. It's a time for mothers to be mothers, this time when darkness gathers. Stories. A song maybe. Plans. An extra blanket, tucked under a child's feet. How many times have I put Erin to bed on the edge of water? Tonight, the salt-drenched air, the smell of hemlock hanging over the bay, the trace of gasoline, the silence, makes me think of so many other nights.

When Erin was young, we camped at the edge of rivers. When the sun dropped low enough to throw the canyon into shadow, I knelt in the doorway of the tent, holding Erin's fuzzy, floppy-footed pajamas. With one hand on each of my shoulders for balance, she put one foot in, then the other, then I zipped her up, one long zipper from her foot to her neck. Then I would pick her up and carry her to the edge of the water. She sat on my lap, or her father's, and we watched nighthawks hunting insects low over the water, swooping skyward until they almost stalled, then dropping to the river, making a sound like a bullfrog. Later, stars cast flicking lights on currents and riffles, and bats came out to hunt. We counted bats together and when we got to ten, it was time for Erin and her brother to go to bed, tucked in a tent with the breeze blowing through.

I thought then that I knew what would happen next. That Erin would grow up and I would grow older. I thought I had it figured—time moves in a linear progression, and no matter how much Erin changed, I would always be twenty-seven years older and that much wiser. But experience sometimes tells against the theories, and the course line is not always the course made good. It never occurred to me that when my daughter grew to be an adult, we would be grown-ups together; that she would learn things I couldn't teach, would love the water even more than I do. It never occurred to me that some day I would look to her to keep me safe. It's okay, I guess. It's good. I'm just surprised is all.

Much later, I'm awakened by a splash and the hollow knock of a kayak against the hull of the boat. Erin's sleeping bag is empty.

The night is black and moonless, the sky dazzling with stars. Wrapping my sweater around my shoulders, I stand up to look over the rail. I can see Erin's silhouette in a kayak, paddling slowly around the star-littered bay. Every time she dips the paddle, glittering light streams off the blade and swirls in the eddy of her stroke. Her bowline glistens where it touches water. Pushing through bioluminescent plankton and jellyfish, the kayak leaves a luminous path in its wake, a hundred galaxies blinking on and off, a million stars sparkling like the Milky Way. My daughter, kayaking on the night sky, so many miles from port.

How astonishing to find ourselves in this place. I know where we began. I know how long we have been going in this direction. Maybe what I didn't understand was how quickly we have traveled.